Ready,
Aim,
Specialize!

Ready,
Aim,
Specialize!

*Create Your Own Writing Specialty
and Make More Money*

BY

KELLY JAMES-ENGER

The Writer Books

The Writer Books is an imprint of Kalmbach Trade Press, a division of Kalmbach Publishing Co. These books are distributed to the book trade by Watson-Guptill.

For all other inquiries, including individual orders or details on special quantity discounts for groups or conferences, contact:

Kalmbach Publishing Co.
21027 Crossroads Circle
Waukesha, WI 53187
(800) 533-6644

Visit our website at http://writermag.com
Secure online ordering available

For feedback on this or any other title by The Writer Books, contact us at this e-mail address: writerbooks@kalmbach.com.

Printed in Canada

02 03 04 05 06 07 08 09 10 11   10 9 8 7 6 5 4 3 2 1

Publisher's Cataloging-in-Publication

    James-Enger, Kelly.
      Ready, aim, specialize! : create your own writing
    specialty and make more money / by Kelly James-Enger.
      p. cm.
      ISBN 0-87116-199-0

      1. Authorship. 2. Freelance journalism—Vocational
    guidance.   I. Title.

PN153.J36 2003   808'.02

To Erik, for holding up the ceiling

ACKNOWLEDGMENTS

I have to admit that as I spent the last few weeks wrapping up this book, I found myself fantasizing about writing the acknowledgments. Not only did it mean I'd be finished with the manuscript (although that was part of it!), but I'd finally get a chance to thank to the many people who have helped, encouraged, and motivated me throughout my writing career. Of course on the tails of that excitement rode the fear that I would inadvertently omit someone. So, as a former lawyer, let me first issue a big, blanket "thank you" to the writers, friends, family, and colleagues who have played a role in my life as a freelancer. Special appreciation to my editors—without you, I would have no freelance career.

Next, I thank the more than fifty writers whom I interviewed for graciously sharing their experience, advice, and wisdom. I could not have written the book without their input: Susanne Alexander, Linda Wasmer Andrews, Cathy Wilkinson Barash, Barbara Bartocci, Tom Bedell, Chuck Bednar, Cindy BeMent, Bob Bittner, Ed Blonz, Melanie Bowden, Tom Brosnahan, Judy Bistany, Polly Campbell, Salvatore Caputo, Sharon Miller Cindrich, Andrea Cooper, Monique Cuvelier, Jackie Dishner, Lain Ehmann, Debbie Elicksen, Leslie Gilbert Elman, Linda Formichelli, Ed Gordon, Susan J. Gordon, Sam Greengard, Tim Harper, Diane Benson Harrington, Leah Ingram, Lisa Iannucci, Joshua Karp, Mary Beth Klatt, Kathy Landis, Kathryn Lay, John Lenger, Joan Lisante, Margaret Littman, Diana Luger, Robert Mark, W. Eric Martin, Janet Mazur, Megan McMorris, JoAnn Milivojevic, Melba Newsome, Nicole Burnham Onsi, Leslie Pepper, Ari Tye Radetsky, Kristin Baird Rattini, Kelly Boyer Sagert, Kathy Sena, Deborah Shouse, Gerry Souter, Sally Stich, Judith Trotsky, Claire Walter, and Arline Zatz.

In particular, several of these writers went above and beyond the call of duty during the months I was working on the book. I'd like to send my extra-special appreciation to:

Polly Campbell, whose enthusiasm, positive attitude, and all-around coolness helped save my freelance career when I was close to giving it up.

Sharon Miller Cindrich, an exceptionally groovy chick and talented essay writer, for her friendship and for reading the final version of this manuscript and making dozens of helpful (and often hilarious) suggestions—all while negotiating an interstate move and the 80 million other things she manages to pull off with seeming effortlessness.

Sam Greengard, for letting me pick his brain endlessly, for reinforcing my idea of what I believe it takes to be a successful freelancer, and for making me laugh as well as educating me about technology writing.

Kris Rattini, my first "freelance friend," for more than four years' worth of e-mails, phone calls, and support—it's been a fabulous ride, my writing buddy!

A few more thank yous are due to these special people as well:

Laurie Harper, my agent, for her hard work on my behalf—I'm looking forward to our next project.

Abby Gnagey, card-maker extraordinaire and smart, talented, and seriously cool chick who never fails to encourage me and point out how far I've come—you rock, too, babe.

My mom, Kathleen James, from whom I inherited my sense of humor, my smarts, and my love for the written word, along with my sweet tooth.

My dad, Dr. Norman E. James, Jr., for being as proud of me as a writer as he was when I was a lawyer.

Cindy Gendry, my separated-at-birth twin, blonde better-half, frequent anecdotal example, and best friend—for all the long lunches and tarot readings, and for making me think that I'm normal (whatever that is).

Ms. Dorothy Vickers-Shelley, my former librarian at Yankee Ridge Elementary School, for inspiring me and encouraging me to write when I was a little girl.

Susan Hanson, my awesome research assistant for this book, who tracked down resources I would have never thought of and without whom I could have never finished this book by the deadline.

Jill Russell, my intern/assistant, a marvelously talented writer whose byline I know I'll see more of in the future.

The wonderful staff at Downers Grove Public Library for letting me pester them with questions and requests over the years—especially the ever-resourceful reference librarians: Amy Johnson Balicki, Lisa Bobbis, Janet Cole, Susan Hanson, Marty Krause, Karen Neal, Bonnie Reid, Lori Sennebogen, Gloria Walsh-Rock, and Carole Zoller; and Barb Baranowski, Debbie Sheehan, Nancy Poch, and Lorel Trout in the interlibrary loan department, who track down obscure journal articles for me without complaint.

The Byliners—Sharon Miller Cindrich, Pat Kocher-Cowan, Lyndee Henderson, Lisa Konkol, and Alida Zamboni—for all the great suggestions, support, and laughter on Monday nights.

And finally, thanks to Erik, my on-site tech-support and help-desk person, who always believed that I could "be a writer" and who has supported me, supplied me with pizzas, back rubs, and M&Ms, and listened patiently when I've been freaked out by having too much work, freaked out by not having enough work, or just freaked out in general. You have made me laugh more times than I can count, and you make my happiness possible.

CONTENTS

Section One: Getting Started

Section Two:
The Top Ten Hottest Specialties

by Elfrieda Abbe

WHEN I FIRST STARTED FREELANCING in Chicago, I took any assignment. For a professional journal for dental students, I wrote about a dentist who cleaned the teeth of gorillas at the zoo. For a refrigeration trade publication, I traipsed around the roof of a 30-story office building to look at an air-conditioning system. On assignment for a city magazine, I rummaged through dozens of antique shops and visited historical buildings in search of stained-glass windows.

My willingness to tackle any subject almost overwhelmed me when I agreed to cover a technical symposium on a German steel-smelting process for *Crain's Chicago Business*. I knew nothing about steel-making. But I was game (and green) enough to take it on because I hoped it would open the door to future assignments.

More interested in the arts than technology, I was out of my element the next day when I walked into a room full of industrialists. The talk was so technical it might as well have been in German. Fortunately, I was sitting next to a sympathetic steel manufacturer, who translated the jargon for me. Later, after some time-consuming background research and fact-checking, I managed to sweat out a ten-inch news story. Given the amount of time I had spent on it, my net earnings were probably in the minus column.

In those early years, I learned the hard way how to find experts, research new topics, find human interest angles, and come up with story ideas. I wrote for everything from newspapers and magazines to trade and professional journals. But I was always having to reinvent the wheel—working with new editors and doing too much research with each new assignment.

I needed a better plan. I needed a strategy.

I needed a book like this one. Kelly James-Enger's *Ready, Aim, Specialize! Create Your Own Writing Specialty and Make More Money* is one of the most useful books for freelance writers that I've read. And it's written by one of the best I know.

Kelly, who is a contributing editor to *The Writer*, is the kind of writer that editors love to work with. Her first query letter caught my attention because she not only had a good story idea, but one particularly well suited to our magazine and on a topic we hadn't yet covered. She had done her homework!

Using her experience writing for fitness magazines, she proposed an article on how to break into that market area. The story came in before the deadline, and it was crisp and clean. Like this book, it was full of useful tips, resources, and concrete examples. Since then, Kelly has written dozens of articles for *The Writer* to help writers plan their career advancement strategies and reach financial goals.

She attributes her own success as a freelance writer to specializing. When she started to concentrate on a handful of topics that interested her—health, fitness, nutrition, and relationships—and began to develop a specialty, she increased her income from $10,000 a year to $90,000. Now, in this book, brimming with enthusiasm, real-life advice, and tons of resources, she outlines how she did it. And tells you how you can, too.

Perhaps you think you don't have a marketable area of expertise. By the end of the first chapter, you'll realize you have three or four. And Kelly will show you how to use what you know to command higher pay rates, save time researching and writing, develop and pitch stories more efficiently, develop relationships with editors, and more.

You'll learn how to get great story ideas and pitch them in that "all-important" document: the query letter. Take it from me as editor of a national magazine that gets constant, countless queries—her advice is sound. Her analysis of the difference between a good query letter and a mediocre one is alone worth the price of this book.

The book also covers ten of today's top specialties. It will help you choose and plan your focus on the market that's right for you.

Kelly's advice is worth following. Her book is an instruction manual for building a successful freelance writing career and becoming an editor's dream.

—Elfrieda Abbe
Editor, *The Writer*

WANT TO MAKE MORE MONEY and set yourself apart from other freelance writers? *Specialize.* That's the theory behind this book, which grew out of my own experience as a full-time freelancer.

Once I developed a specialty of my own (actually, several of them), I found that assignments came easier, my productivity increased, and my income quadrupled—all because I concentrated on a handful of subjects rather than trying to write about anything and everything.

To help you learn why you should—and how you can—specialize as a freelancer, this book is divided into three sections:

Section One: Getting Started. This section explains the basics of how and why you should specialize. In Chapters 1 and 2, it explains why to consider developing a niche of your own. Chapter 3 reviews effective marketing and research techniques. And Chapter 4 gives an overview of the article-writing process from the first kernel of an idea to seeing your work in print.

Section Two: The Top Ten Hottest Specialties. This section offers ten chapters, each dedicated to a nonfiction writing specialty. Each chapter includes a brief overview of writing for that particular niche, followed by plenty of practical advice from writers who work in the field, potential markets for articles, and a useful batch of resources: organizations, Web sites, books, and more. Each chapter also includes a Tale from the Front—dos and don'ts from a successful freelancer in this area.

Afterword: Beyond Article Writing. This section offers a chapter that describes how to branch out into other fields and maximize your income and productivity. It is followed by a brief appendix that lists additional books, organizations, and market sources of note.

Every writer has his or her own reasons for freelancing, but I think it's safe to say that most would like to make more money doing it . . . or, at the very least, wouldn't mind increasing their cash flow. This book will help you do that.

Whether you freelance as a hobby or full-time, why not earn a lucrative income from it as well? *Ready, Aim, Specialize!* will help you expand your writing career—by narrowing your focus.

—Kelly James-Enger

P.S. Your feedback is greatly appreciated! If you have any comments on this book (about anything you found especially helpful, or follow-up questions you might have), or if you have suggestions of your own on how other writers might improve their freelance careers, please drop me a note at this e-mail address: writerbooks@kalmbach.com.

CHAPTER 1

Why Specialize?

WHEN YOU EMBARKED ON your writing career, what were your dreams? I'd venture to guess that you loved to write, and hoped you could publish your work and get paid something for it. The idea that you could make a good living by writing full-time—or have your writing become a very profitable sideline—may not have even occurred to you early on.

How do I know this? Because I remember how I used to think. When I launched my freelance career in January 1997, my goals were modest. I wanted to make enough money that I wouldn't have to return to practicing law. I had no idea of what to expect (more about that later), but I thought if I could eventually make $15,000 or even as much as $20,000 a year as a freelancer, I'd be thrilled. If you had told me then that I could make $90,000 a year writing for magazines, I would have never believed you.

But I do earn that much now. And I've never been happier.

For many writers and would-be writers, the idea of freelancing full-time—and making a good living doing it—is a long-standing dream. As a freelancer, you are your own boss. You no longer have to worry about commuting, dress codes, marathon office meetings, or gossipy coworkers. Instead of set hours, your time is your own. You control how much or how little you work. You lounge about in comfortable clothes, take occasional breaks for a cup of coffee or a brief stroll, and write when the muse appears. You take days off whenever you like, and generally live a relaxed, creative, self-fulfilled, stress-free existence. (Black turtlenecks optional.)

At least that's how many would-be writers imagine their freelancing lives. However, the reality can be disillusioning. While freelance writing offers many great benefits, you also confront clients who take months to pay, editors who solicit query ideas and then never respond to them, feast-or-famine work cycles, and a complete lack of benefits, vacation time, and sick days, not to mention the constant isolation.

Ask most people who write full-time, and they'll tell you they're not doing it for the money. In fact, a survey conducted by the National Writers' Union in 1995 confirmed this—the median income for freelancing was only $4,000 a year, and only 16 percent of freelancers surveyed made more than $30,000 a year.

However, those statistics hide that fact that freelancers who choose the right path are much more likely to succeed and make the kind of living that the writers (myself included) whose advice is presented in this book are able to earn consistently.

The Know-Nothing Freelancer: My Story

When I quit my demanding career as a lawyer to write full-time, I didn't know about the supposedly bleak financial future I was facing, and I'm not sure whether these dismal numbers would have scared me off. To be honest, I had no idea what I was getting into. Although I'd majored in rhetoric in college and fantasized about "being a writer" (haven't we all?) for much of my life, I had no working knowledge of the freelance lifestyle.

At the time I escaped the law, I had never spoken to or even seen a freelance writer (at least not to my knowledge) and had no concept of what exactly self-employed writers did all day—other than write, of course.

I was, however, extremely motivated. Although I'd managed to scrimp together six months' worth of expenses to live on, I knew I'd have to nail paying assignments immediately to be able to continue doing it full-time. I also knew I didn't want to go back to practicing law. That gave me six months to get my writing career off the ground.

So, from the outset, I was always as concerned with my bottom line as I was with the quality of my writing. I'd written short fiction and poetry for years, but I realized there weren't many high-paying markets for this kind of writing. Instead, I decided to focus on writing nonfiction magazine articles.

In the previous year, I'd managed to sell two stories, one to *Cosmopolitan* and one to *Bride's*. At the time, I knew nothing about the rules of the game—that you were supposed to write queries first, for example, instead of sending in completed manuscripts. (Duh!) I churned out articles on a variety of topics and dashed them off to magazines that seemed to fit the subject matter and tone. (While I supported the U.S. Postal Service by doing so, not many of these early articles sold—more on this later.)

Writing as a sideline had netted me a couple of decent checks, but if I was going to write full-time, I needed a financial goal to shoot for. My first year, it was a modest one—$10,000. I still can't remember why I chose that figure, other than the fact that it was a nice, neat sum. If I could make $10,000 from freelancing my first year, I thought, then maybe I could succeed in this new career I'd chosen. (I didn't realize that my goal was more than twice the median amount that freelancers make—I suppose ignorance really is bliss.)

But while I had this dollar figure as my goal, I didn't concern myself with how I would achieve it. My strategy was simply to write articles, query madly, and take every writing assignment that came my way as long as it paid.

And I did just about everything my first year. I wrote brochures for local companies for a few hundred dollars. I "strung" for the local paper and produced features that paid between $35 and $75, and wrote real estate "advertorials" (sales pieces that described specific properties) for $50 each. I took on an educational consulting job where I produced career materials and spoke to grade-school students about their future jobs, and I did copywriting for a local hospital for $35/hour. In the meantime, I queried magazines with story ideas and occasionally sent out essays and completed articles as well.

When it came to magazines, my approach at the time was to look for story ideas and then find the appropriate markets for those articles. In between dozens of rejections, some magazine assignments trickled in. *Bride's* assigned me another piece, this time on combining two households into one when you marry. *Vegetarian Times* asked me to write a 600-word story on creating a local vegetarian group. *Complete Woman* bought my light piece on ten reasons to date "shy guys." I wrote about a unique high-school paper for *Editor & Publisher*, and about a martial-arts expert who teaches self-defense classes to people with physical limitations for *Accent on Living*. *The Lion* asked me to cover a charity car show sponsored by the local Lions club after I pitched the idea to them.

So far, so good. During this time, I had no intention of specializing in any particular area. I wrote about any idea that I thought would fit a particular market and bring me some cash. It didn't matter to me if I was writing about charity car shows, one-on-one marketing techniques, or animal research; I only cared about the assignment, the clip, and the check—and rightly so. With my limited experience, I couldn't afford to be too choosy about work. I needed to build my portfolio and gain experience—after all, I had no journalism background and was basically learning the ropes by trial and error.

Creating a Niche . . . by Accident

But there were trade-offs. Although I was slowly amassing clips, I was also spending long hours reviewing possible magazine markets, researching potential story ideas, and writing compelling query letters. I might spend a day or more gathering information and writing up a query that would then be rejected; in the meantime, I was busily pitching as many magazines as I possibly could. At one point, I had 54 query letters, completed articles, and essays circulating in the mail. But from a percentage standpoint, not many of these queries or articles were selling.

This is what I now call the "saturation-bombing technique"—simply sending out as many articles and queries as you can manage. You figure, hey, if I get enough stuff out there, something will happen.

I fell victim to this belief early on. I'd lie in bed at night and read market guides like *Writer's Market* and *The Writer's Handbook*. If a magazine paid well (and sadly, that was often my only consideration), I'd whip up a query or an article, often without even bothering to look at the magazine itself. Guess what? Though I sent out hundreds of queries the first couple of years, I've never sold to a market that I didn't actually read first—even though I could have easily acquired a sample issue from the publisher simply by writing and requesting a copy.

Not surprisingly, considering the number of queries and articles I was churning out, I was getting burned out within the first eight months of my fledgling writing career. I was working mornings, afternoons, evenings, and most weekends—pretty much the same way I had as a lawyer. Researching so many different types of story ideas and trying to keep up with dozens of different markets was taking its toll. I was tired, cranky, and rapidly losing enthusiasm for the idea of "being a writer." There had to be an easier way.

And, it turned out, there was. Rather than trying to cover a wide variety of subjects, I started to concentrate on a handful of topics that interested me and were a part of my life—health, fitness, nutrition, and relationships—and began developing a specialty in those areas.

In the years since then, I've met hundreds of other freelance writers, and I have discovered that the majority of the ones who make a good living freelancing full-time (say, earning more than $30,000 a year) have created niches for themselves.

Maybe they write about fitness and health. Or business and technology. Or food and nutrition. Or home and garden. Rather than being generalists, they're now specializing in specific areas, and reaping the benefits of doing so.

As you'll see in the pages and chapters to come, creating a nonfiction specialty can enable writers to:

- Command higher per-word rates.

- Save time researching and writing articles.

- Develop and pitch timely story ideas more efficiently.

- Position themselves as experts on certain topics.

- Obtain assignments from higher-paying markets.

- Develop relationships with editors.

- Create an inventory of stories for reprinting and reselling.

- Break into new subject areas.

My first specialty came about unintentionally. After selling two articles to *Bride's*, I'd developed a list of other possible wedding-related story ideas. When *Bride's* turned them down, I pitched some of them to *Bridal Guide*. Based on my clips and ideas, the editor at *Bridal Guide* assigned one. That led to another story for that magazine, and then another; in the meantime, I queried some of the remaining rejected ideas to *For the Bride by Demetrios* and started picking up assignments there as well.

In a matter of months, I'd turned two bridal articles into a specialty of sorts. Since then, I've written more than 25 stories for bridal magazines, many of which have been reprinted at least once, and am now a contributing editor at *For the Bride.*

Fellow attorney and freelance writer Nicole Burnham Onsi developed her bridal niche by accident as well. "I'm a romance writer, and the first nonfiction magazine story I wrote was a piece about romance writers for *Boston Magazine.* Since it was my only clip, I asked myself what markets might look favorably on that clip. Then I tried to 'package' myself accordingly," says Onsi. "I thought that since I was a new bride and had a story about romance as a clip, I might try pitching stories to bridal magazines. I read through several, studying what kinds of angles their articles took, and sent off queries."

Her research paid off—her first query to *Bride's* resulted in an assignment. Since then, she's written about 50 bridal-related articles. Specializing has cut the time she spends pitching new story ideas; this gives her more time to work on her third romance novel and take care of her two young children. "Having a niche makes getting assignments within that market much easier," says Onsi. "The editors know who I am, and I can pitch article ideas via e-mail. I don't have to mail out piles of clips, or send ultra-detailed outlines or query letters. That's a big time-saver."

From Fat to Fit: Another Niche Is Created

I've been interested in fitness and diet topics since college, partly due to the fact that I managed to gain a whopping 45 pounds my freshman year. (This was the period my mother euphemistically refers to as "when there was more of you to love.") I'd been a competitive swimmer in high school, and ate to fuel myself for long workouts. When I started college, I quit swimming—but kept eating the way I had before. When I realized I had outgrown my summer clothes, I started running and counting calories to lose the extra weight, which led to a long-standing interest in nutrition and exercise. Over the years, I've continued to work out regularly and also became a vegetarian.

My first fitness-related sale was to *Shape*; I pitched a story on how to maintain your fitness routine when you relocate. Because I'd moved four times in five years, I was uniquely qualified to write the piece, and I incorporated my firsthand experience into the lead. That clip helped me get my first assignment for *Fit*, on how to determine your exercise personality. This soon led to other articles for my editor at *Fit* on topics including exercise addiction, easy ways to eat better, and potential dieting dangers. In the meantime, I pitched new story ideas to *Fitness* and wrote a number of workout articles for that publication as well.

Although I hadn't intended to specialize in fitness and diet topics, it was starting to pay off. First, I was finding it easier to come up with story ideas because I was writing about subjects that interested and directly affected me. My own experiences and those of friends and family often inspired article ideas.

After I broke my ankle and had to take six weeks off from running, I turned to a heart-rate monitor to help me get back in shape. That turned into a story ("Target Your Training," *Fit*). My sister-in-law was diagnosed with sleep apnea after fighting fatigue for months. That turned into a story ("Tired of Being Tired?" *Woman's Day*). After I was forced to wait ten minutes to use an abdominal machine at the gym (this woman refused to relinquish her seat!), I realized I had the perfect lead for a query—and that turned into a story as well! ("The Top Ten Gym Sins," *Fit*).

The second advantage was that I was spending less time researching these topics. For example, when writing an exercise story, I knew what the personal trainer meant when she talked about targeting your "lats." When a physician quoted a figure from the "CDC," I knew he meant the Centers for Disease Control. And if a dietitian mentioned the benefits of consuming omega-3 fats, I didn't have to ask what exactly those were. The more I wrote about these topics, the deeper my knowledge became and the easier it was to research and compose the final stories. I was also developing a Rolodex of experts to whom I could turn for interviews or when I just needed to quickly confirm a fact or nab a quote.

Megan McMorris has worked as an editor at magazines including *Fit* and *Fitness*; she's now a freelancer based in Portland, Oregon, whose stories have appeared in magazines including *Fitness, Self, Sports Illustrated for Women*, and *Glamour*. She says her lifelong interest in fitness was the jumping-off point for her magazine writing and editing career, and agrees there are many benefits to having a writing niche.

"For one thing, after doing so many fitness-related articles, I feel like I've become somewhat of a 'mini' expert myself. And therefore I don't have to research nearly as much as I would if the topic was completely foreign to me, which makes it easier," says McMorris.

"Another positive," she says, "to having a niche is that when I get an assignment, I already have plenty of contacts in the fitness field, many of whom remember me from previous articles. So it's very easy to get interviews. I don't have to spend time researching who the top experts are, because I already know them."

Her knowledge of fitness-related topics has also helped her get first-time assignments from magazines she hasn't written for before. In fact, many editors approach her with article opportunities.

The Financial Payoff

But the unforeseen bonus when I started to specialize was a major increase in my income. As I established myself as a freelancer with a background in fitness and later in health and nutrition, I became more valuable to the editors I worked for. My

Explore Other Areas

By diversifying, I've increased my income potential and also created a way to keep things fun, lively, and interesting for me on a daily basis. I think if I was writing about weddings or parenting 100 percent of the time, I would grow bored with the topic.

But by having a variety of projects going at once, I can pick and choose which ones I work on based on how I'm feeling that day.

I really think that diversifying is key—hey, it's just like your investment portfolio. Your financial adviser wouldn't suggest that you put all of your investment eggs in one basket. Why should your freelance career be any different?
—Leah Ingram, New Hope, Pennsylvania

average per-word rates started to rise. One magazine that had paid me 50 cents/word agreed to raise my rate to 75 cents/word. This meant an additional $250 for a 1,000-word article.

Another boosted my fee from $1 to $1.25/word. A third offered me $1.35/word for my first health story because the editor knew I'd written other health and fitness articles. I was discovering that most markets are willing to pay more to writers who come equipped with a background in the area they're writing about.

Corporate pilot and freelancer Rob Mark of Evanston, Illinois, first started writing about aviation subjects. However, he quickly realized that knowing about related areas would make him a more effective researcher and writer. He spent time learning about business, marketing, and technology subjects to help set him apart from other freelancers. "When someone starts talking about something on an aviation story that is very business-focused, for example, you need to be conversant enough in that language that you can talk the talk," says Mark. "And when the person you're interviewing realizes that you can speak or understand some of the lingo that is important to them, it puts them at ease. Furthermore, if you have some experience in these areas, you can ask biting questions you might not even think of if you didn't know a whole lot about business or technology."

Mark's experience has also allowed him to negotiate higher rates. "When you have editors who can just give you the story and let you run with it, that shows a lot of confidence. It certainly speaks to the issue of where they place you on their writer hierarchy," says Mark. "And in some cases, it's allowed me to pull more money out of certain stories—because they know I can do that."

It makes sense. If editors know that you'll do a good job, it saves them hassles and headaches, which is usually worth a few more dollars to them.

Finding New Markets

Another benefit of specializing is that it enables writers to break into markets that might otherwise be closed to them. While I hadn't written for any parenting magazines, I wanted to break into this field, so I pitched some women's health ideas to an editor at *Parents*. I used a similar approach—suggesting some health and fitness-related story ideas—to query *RxRemedy*, a publication aimed at 50-plus readers. Both stories were assigned because of my health-writing experience.

Writers can also develop specialties based on their work histories. Lain Ehmann, a freelancer in Los Gatos, California, found that her previous work experience paid off when she began her freelance writing career. "I came to freelance writing with a background in high-tech public relations and marketing," says Ehmann. "My first pieces were in the high-tech arena. I didn't get pigeonholed, per se. I just found the opportunities there to be plentiful."

She admits that the work isn't always fascinating, but the pay makes it worthwhile. "I've quit fighting the fact that I'm so well suited to write about business and technology," she explains. "I used to long to do something different. But now I recognize that I bring to the table almost ten years in high-tech experience— and editors are willing to pay dearly for that."

While Ehmann has branched out into other fields including parenting and health, she says it's her niche that sets her apart from other writers and brings in the most income. "It's impossible to keep track of everything that's going on in the world, and to be a valuable writer (especially when you're breaking into a market), you have to know who's who, what's new, and what's old. The only way to do that is to specialize to some degree," says Ehmann. "I'm not saying you only have to write about integrated circuits. But if you choose to specialize in a few fields, your job of staying on top of the trends and the people will be that much easier."

Multiple Specialties

Just because you specialize doesn't mean you're limited to one field. Linda Formichelli, a freelancer in the Boston area, has multiple niches including business, health/nutrition, career, pets, and writing for kids.

"I seem to have fallen into each of these niches. Once I sold a single article in one of these areas, I was able to use that article as a clip to get more work in the field," says Formichelli. "The reason that I have so many niches is that when I brainstorm ideas, I'm not constrained by field—I'm all over the place! In one session I may come up with an idea for *Wired* and an idea for *Family Circle*—both of which I've written for.

"I have so many niches that I consider myself a generalist. But within each of those niches, I find it easier to get work because I can show editors plenty of clips to prove that I know my stuff," she continues. "Those clips also make it easier to get into the top magazines, so I earn higher rates."

Kristin Baird Rattini, a freelancer who currently lives in Shanghai, China, turned a one-time opportunity into ongoing work assignments from a number of corporate magazines. "The old 'who you know' got me my break into corporate publications. A high-school friend was communications director for a Midwestern telecommunications company," says Rattini. "She needed new writers for the company's quarterly in-house magazine, so she called. Those clips in turn helped me land work with *True Value*, *IGA Grocergram*, and *Correspondent*, a magazine put out by Aid Association for Lutherans."

Rattini didn't intend to develop another niche in consumer finance, but had queried the Credit Union National Association with her corporate clips. "The editor liked my style, so she gave me work on CUNA's consumer finance publications," says Rattini. "That was three years and several dozen assignments ago. I've since become well versed on credit cards, mortgages, investing, and other consumer finance topics."

Of course, not every successful nonfiction writer has a specialty or even wants one. Take W. Eric Martin, a freelancer in the Boston area, who considers himself a generalist who writes well about most topics. "I write regularly for a number of trade magazines—several in the printing industry, for example—but don't feel I've carved out a niche," says Martin. "I still know next to nothing about the printing industry (albeit more than a random person off the street). So I write mostly profiles, which require little in the way of in-depth knowledge."

Part of his problem, he says, is a lack of markets for the subjects that he has a stronger background in. "The fields that I really am interested in and have some knowledge of (mathematics, games, fiction) lack publications that pay decent wages, so there's little hope of translating that knowledge into a writing career," says Martin. "Instead I write about printers, KFC operators, and regular people who lower their sugar and cholesterol consumption—and I spend my spare time on topics I enjoy."

Get Ready to Specialize

For most freelancers, though, developing one or more niches—especially in areas that feature hundreds of potential markets—can pay off in a variety of ways. In the chapters that follow, you'll explore some of the highest-paying and hottest nonfiction specialties. And you'll learn how to turn your unique background and experience into one or more specialties, increasing your freelance income in the process.

You'll discover the dos and don'ts of writing about each area from freelancers who cover those topics. And you'll get an idea of the types of markets that buy and publish these kinds of stories.

Finally, you'll find organizations, associations, Web sites, and other resources that will be invaluable as you begin to carve out a specialty of your own.

CHAPTER 2

Getting Started

What You Need to Specialize

OKAY, SO YOU NOW HAVE AN IDEA of why it's worth your while to specialize. The next question becomes: What exactly will you specialize in?

Think back to what you first wrote about. Many freelancers break into the field by pitching subjects that they're familiar with. The same was true for me. My first article sale was to *Cosmopolitan* magazine. I wrote a service-oriented piece about how to survive your last two weeks at a job after you've given your notice. I had firsthand experience with this subject—as an unhappy lawyer, I had changed firms several times during my short career, each time hoping the new job would be the right fit for me.

My friends and I had also commiserated about the misery of those final days—*you* know you don't want to be there, and *they* know you don't want to be there. It's a tense, uncomfortable experience for nearly everyone. Many times during those last two weeks, I had to bite my tongue to keep from saying things like "You'll miss me when I'm gone," or "You have no idea how much I've hated working here," or similar bridge-burning comments. I figured other *Cosmo* readers would relate to this topic . . . and they did.

My legal background also gave me the idea for my second published article—a story for *Bride's* on how engaged couples can avoid legal problems as they plan their weddings. I was engaged at the time I wrote it, and was amazed at how many unscrupulous vendors I ran into. Several reception hall owners, for example, dodged questions about how much liability insurance they carried, and two refused to put bids in writing. One particularly sleazy guy even told me that I "didn't need to worry myself about things like that." Little did he know that as a contract lawyer, I was trained to worry about "things like that." Luckily I knew better than to hire any of these people, but I also realized how easily another bride could be—and often is—taken advantage of in this situation.

The eventual article, "Promises, Promises," gave engaged couples practical ways to protect themselves and avoid potential legal problems, drawing on my experience both as an attorney and as a bride. The editor who bought it told me that I'd done a good job of dispensing legal advice in straightforward, easy-to-understand language. "Most of the articles we get from attorneys and accountants are way too complicated, and full of legalese and jargon," she said. "But yours is perfect for our audience."

Don't Think You're an Expert?

Contrary to what you might think, you needn't be an M.D. or other recognized "expert" to focus your writing in a particular area. Your educational background, life experience, and interest in certain subjects can all be translated into a writing-related specialty. When I teach magazine writing, I have students write down at least five things about their lives that they have specialized knowledge of or interest in. Make a list of your own, to get

Set Your Own Standards

You can't go by everyone else's standards; it's a recipe for mediocrity. There's no reason why you can't make $200,000 a year writing.

I made $275,000 in 2000 and $215,000 in 2001, even in a slow economy. If I went by what everyone else said, that wouldn't be possible.

Anything is possible if you set your mind to it and if you work to achieve it.

—Sam Greengard, Burbank, California

yourself started thinking about what you bring to the table when you pitch a story.

For example, have you traveled the world? Lived in different parts of the United States? Raised children? Dealt with a chronic medical condition?

Are you an avid gardener? Do you cook from scratch and have the ability to whip up fantastic dinners in 30 minutes' time?

Have you run your own business? Do you have firsthand knowledge of a particular industry, trade, or profession? What are your hobbies?

Have you volunteered for a church, school, or nonprofit organization?

Who are your friends, family members, coworkers, and colleagues? What sorts of specialized knowledge do they have?

Use this space to create a list of your own:

I have specialized knowledge about:

_____

_____

_____

_____

My work background includes the following subjects:

_____

_____

_____

_____

My hobbies and interests include the following:

_____

_____

_____

_____

I know or have access to people who have expertise in the following areas:

_____

_____

_____

_____

I'm interested in the following subjects:

_____

_____

_____

_____

In my life, I'm currently dealing with these issues:

_____

_____

_____

_____

Creating a list of these subjects will often trigger story ideas and will also give you an inkling of the many areas in which you have a background that other writers may not.

For example, when I created a list of my own in a recent workshop for writers, I came up with the following:

- My dad is a dentist.

- I've been a runner for 15 years.

- My sister is a police officer.

- I'm a vegetarian.

- I'm a lawyer.

Even a quick look at this list proves that I do have specialized knowledge I can use when pitching and writing articles. Granted, there's probably not a huge demand for articles about vegetarian attorneys, but I do know more about teeth than the average person. Not only is my dad a dentist, but my mom worked at his office for years, and I even had a brief stint as a dental receptionist there between college and law school.

In some families, they notice a person's clothing or jewelry or cars. My parents notice teeth. (Think I'm joking? It's not unusual for my mom to comment on how one of her neighbors should "really get that overbite fixed." In my family, "he has the nicest teeth" is high praise indeed.) This doesn't mean that I'm a dental expert by any means, but when I was writing about canker sores (also known as "oral aphthous ulcers") and had a question, my dad was only a phone call away.

If I have basic questions about law enforcement or how the arresting and booking system works, I can ask my sister. Are you really entitled to a phone call?—or is that just something I've picked up from cop shows? Maybe I'll pitch an article on how to avoid getting a speeding ticket, or what a homeowner can do to reduce the risk of becoming a victim of crime. How can you prevent having your purse snatched? What's the best way to handle someone who harasses you on the street? My sister Stephie can answer these questions and lead me to other experts or sources of information I might not otherwise know about.

And of course, as a long-term runner I've had no shortage of story ideas. I've written about using heart-rate monitors, stretching for flexibility, how to maintain your exercise motivation, and how your eating habits can help you get more out of your workouts. The fact that I pay attention to what I eat (and eventually became a vegetarian) led to stories about easy ways to eat better, overcoming the biggest diet pitfalls, the negative emotional consequences of constant dieting, and a slew of weight-loss stories. No, I'm not a fitness or nutrition expert per se, but my long-standing interest in both subjects and personal experience give me a depth of knowledge that the average writer simply doesn't have. Can I call it a specialty? Sure.

Some life experiences naturally lend themselves to a slew of article ideas. Parenting is one such area. Janet Mazur, a freelancer in Ocean Grove, New Jersey, was a newspaper reporter and a magazine writer/editor in the United States. She'd also freelanced while living abroad and had worked for major daily papers in Sydney and Melbourne, Australia, writing general features. But she never gave parenting writing a thought—until she became a parent herself.

"It seemed a logical transition," says Mazur. "And frankly, I've written partially for selfish purposes when it comes to parenting. There are so many things I wanted to know and explore—as a new mom, at home by choice, I yearned to connect with other women in the same boat." Mazur's first parenting story was a feature for a newspaper on how new moms could hook up with each other. The story addressed their desire for connection, the unexpected loneliness of staying at home with a new baby, and the depression women sometimes experience as a result.

Since then, Mazur has found her daughter to be an inexhaustible supply of story ideas. "It is one of the unexpected bonuses of having children and being a writer—a gift, really," says Mazur. "They are an easy source, an endless well of ideas, because they change and grow all the time. Their 'issues' are always in flux."

For example, when her daughter was a toddler with a

"blankie," Mazur wrote a story explaining the purpose of such comfort objects, using her child as the lead. As her daughter grew, Mazur wrote about developmental issues like spitting up and skin ailments. Later, she produced articles aimed at parents of school-aged kids—like what to do when your child starts hanging out with the neighborhood "bad kids."

Sharon Cindrich, who lives in Wauwatosa, Wisconsin, started her freelance career after she had children. The former graphic designer and copywriter had fantasized about being a full-time writer—because "it seemed romantic and glamorous!" she says with a laugh. She started writing essays, only to have them rejected. After taking a class in essay writing, she polished her skills and sold her first piece to the Woman News section of the *Chicago Tribune*. Since then, she's sold dozens of essays and now is a regular columnist for *Western Suburban Living*, a regional magazine, and a local paper.

Cindrich has also branched out into writing articles for magazines and Web sites, but she's chosen to focus on family, health, and parenting issues. "It's always easier. I'm already an expert of sorts because most of the things I write about are issues in my own life," says Cindrich. "Because of that, I can reach people and pass on information more effectively than if I didn't know it as well."

Creating Your Specialty

If you already have experience in a particular industry, you can use that as a stepping-stone to other fields as well. Joan Lisante, an attorney based in Oakton, Virginia, started her freelance career by publishing a humorous essay on what she calls "real-life Barbies" in several newspapers. She then realized her legal background gave her a unique perspective that she could sell to editors when pitching business and legal topics. She now specializes in writing about business and legal topics, and has branched out to cover medical and technical issues, too.

While some writers intend to specialize, other simply fall into niches that complement their backgrounds and skills. Kathy Sena of Manhattan Beach, California, was a technical writer and editor who freelanced on the side. In 1994 she started freelancing full-time. After developing specialties in health and lifestyle topics, like Mazur she moved into the parenting arena when her son was born.

"I write two syndicated health columns for United Parenting Publications, a group of 27 regional parenting magazines. And that has helped me break into other markets such as the *L.A. Times* health section and *Shape* magazine," says Sena. "In addition to getting more assignments, I'm able to get higher rates. Also, when you specialize, you tend to more quickly build up a Rolodex full of great contacts—which leads to more article ideas and more work."

Specializing by Choice

Some writers choose to specialize to set themselves apart from others in the field. Melba Newsome, a freelancer in Matthews, North Carolina, was working full-time as a paralegal in Los Angeles when she decided to start writing. She found the process frustrating at first. "I kept getting rejected or heard nothing back at all. I got absolutely nowhere sending out service or health ideas," says Newsome. "Then I pitched true-life stories. I got my first assignment for a national magazine (*Family Circle*) with a true-life story. I realized that I had a much better batting average with these types of stories."

Newsome decided to focus on finding the stories that editors wouldn't be able to come up with on their own. "It was clear that so many of the lifestyle or general-interest ideas were generated in-house. But there was no one at the editorial meetings saying, 'I have a great story about a woman who was in a harem for six months!'" she explains. "They needed writers on the ground and outside of New York for that. That was me!"

Give Your Editors What They Want

A characteristic of successful freelancers—something they don't tell you in books or at conferences—is that they keep their editors happy.

They make their editors' jobs easier.

My editors like me because I never miss a deadline, I turn in clean copy, and when they ask for changes, I do them.

I sometimes argue with changes, of course, but the bottom line is this: the editor is the boss.

If I don't like the way an editor is handling a story, I still give the editor what he or she wants on that story.

I might not work with him or her again, but on every assignment, I try to satisfy that editor.

—Tim Harper, Ridgewood, New Jersey

In the years since then, she's written more than 50 true-life stories for magazines including *Cosmopolitan*, *Marie Claire*, *Essence*, *Good Housekeeping*, and *Family Circle*. The fact that she's willing to do some digging and come up with unique stories has kept her in demand.

"Editors want writers who can generate a steady stream of ideas. It saves them time and a lot of hassle," says Newsome. "I try to set myself apart by finding the greatest story subjects. Of course, this means watching a lot of trash TV and reading a lot of sleazy stories.

"One editor told me that I was the exception by far. I was one of the few writers they had who came up with their own ideas. Otherwise, most were generated in-house—which meant they were constantly brainstorming and scrambling for ideas. Having someone say, 'Here are three stories,' makes her life easier."

Bob Bittner of Charlotte, Michigan, is creating a niche for himself writing about animals, a long-term interest of his. "I wanted to break into *Family Circle*. And I wanted to develop a specialty writing about animals and pets—yes, we have two cats," says Bittner.

"I had noticed that *Family Circle* ran a regular pets column, so I thought that was a good place to pitch, rather than trying to break in with an investigative health piece or a "Women Who Make a Difference" story. Also, I figured that they'd get fewer well-targeted (and fresh) ideas for that section, so mine would really stand out. I must have done something right. My first pitch resulted in an assignment."

Bob's first story was about how to find and evaluate a good pet sitter, and he's written three pet articles for *Family Circle* since then. With those clips in hand, he's now branching out. "I'm mapping out a path to some of my dream markets, broadening my interest in animals and pets to include nature and conservation," he says. "For me, it's a matter of wanting to make a living writing about things that interest me. So, following those interests results in developing a variety of specialties."

Freelancer Sam Greengard of Burbank, California, wrote for a variety of national consumer magazines—about "pretty much anything and everything"—until the early 1990s. "At that point, I recognized that there was a huge opportunity in business and technology writing, so I made a conscious effort to focus there," says Greengard. "I never told anyone that I wouldn't work for them. I simply stopped pitching editors in the general-interest arena and began focusing on business and technology. It probably took about three to four years to really take off.

"Over the years, you conduct interviews, you read the trade magazines, you read material on the Internet, and you develop a pretty strong body of knowledge," says Greengard. "By specializing, I don't have to reinvent the wheel every time or research a topic I know nothing about. Chances are I know something about it—and I know enough to ask the right questions."

Will you create a specialty from the outset? Or will you choose a niche after a few years, once you've had a chance to write about a variety of topics?

The choice is yours. Either way, by pitching yourself as a writer with a unique background and specialized knowledge, you'll boost your profile with editors and increase the likelihood that you'll be offered an assignment.

And in today's marketplace, with so many writers competing for stories, that factor can only work to your advantage.

Believe in Youself

You have to be self-confident and believe that you can do the job.

I run into a lot of writers who just don't think their work is worth appearing in a national magazine . . . or it's only worth $1/word . . . or they wouldn't dream of touching a contract.

If you're confident in your abilities and in yourself, you will seek what your work is worth. You will step up to better paying markets. You will negotiate better contracts.

And ultimately, you will be a more successful freelancer—regardless of how you define success.

—Bob Bittner, Charlotte, Michigan

CHAPTER 3

Tricks of the Trade

Queries & Research Techniques

WHETHER YOU WRITE ABOUT A VARIETY of sub-jects or specialize in just a few areas, the basics of freelancing still apply. To be a successful nonfiction writer, you must be able to develop compelling story ideas, find markets for your work, pitch ideas to editors, conduct research, find and interview experts and other sources, and write accurately and well—all this while meeting deadlines and finding ways to make your editors' and clients' jobs easier.

Developing Compelling Story Ideas

"Where do you get your ideas, anyway?"

How many times have you been asked this question? What nonwriters don't realize is that the problem isn't coming up with ideas—there are millions of them floating around. The harder, more time-consuming part is taking an idea, coming up with an interesting or newsworthy angle, tweaking it for a particular market, and proving that it's timely, interesting, and important to the publication you're pitching.

When I started freelancing, I looked for—and found—ideas everywhere. But an idea by itself isn't enough. I had to decide what angle to take with the story and then select the markets that I thought would be most interested in the piece.

I looked for story ideas that impacted my life or those of my friends, family members, and neighbors. I also searched for local ideas that editors in New York or other cities might not have access to—this is a great way to get your foot in the door with a publication.

Tracking trends is another way to come up with ideas. For instance, simplifying and downsizing your life, a growing trend in the 1990s, continues to be big. Likewise, interest in complementary and alternative medicine remains strong, and should continue to be as the baby boomers age. Harnessing technology to save time at work or home is of ongoing interest.

And many topics are timeless. Staying healthy. Being financially secure. Finding and keeping a romantic partner. Raising smart, self-assured, healthy kids. Succeeding at your chosen career. Living a life that seems to have a purpose to it.

Think of what's important to you and those around you, and you'll have no shortage of ideas.

The All-Important Query Letter

The usual way to pitch an idea to an editor is with a query letter. Its importance cannot be overstated. The query serves a three-part purpose. It's your letter of introduction, your sales pitch, and your initial and most important writing sample. Every query showcases your writing ability; it should also demonstrate your familiarity with the market itself and convince the editor that you are the perfect person to write the story.

There is no magic formula for writing queries, but most free-lancers develop a rough template that they can use as a model

Save Time Querying

I put together packets of my clips in advance—complete with my card and an SASE—and stick it all in a mailing envelope with my return address.

Then, when I go to send a query, I don't waste time gathering the pieces together . . . and looking for a stamp for the SASE.

It's all ready to go. All I need to add is my query letter, and it's off.

—Sharon Miller Cindrich, Wauwatosa, Wisconsin

for future letters. I like a basic four-paragraph structure that includes the following elements:

- The lead—to capture the editor's attention.

- Development of the story idea—i.e., why write it?

- "Nuts and bolts"—a working title, potential sources, word count, sidebars, etc.

- Why me?—the "I-am-so-great" paragraph. Don't be shy about describing your qualifications and experience.

I confess that when I started freelancing, I would often start queries with the snooze-inducing language, "I'm a freelancer and I am writing you because I would like to write an article about . . ." Think about it. When you read an article in a newspaper or magazine, the story doesn't start out by saying, "This will be an article on how reducing the fat in your diet can improve your health . . ." No, the article grabs your attention with a statistic, an interesting fact, a recent study, or an anecdote. Your query should start out with the same kind of lead.

The second paragraph is where you prove your case to the editor and demonstrate why the story should be written. You might mention a time peg that explains the story's relevance. You may include eye-catching statistics or describe how this topic will impact readers' lives. How many people are affected by the subject you want to write about? How will readers benefit from this piece? Remember, the editor wants to sell magazines, so you should be thinking the way she does. She's wondering whether this particular story will motivate someone standing in line at the grocery store or browsing through hundreds of periodicals at Borders or Barnes & Noble to pick up and purchase this particular issue of her magazine. You want to convince her that it will. (Many editors think of "cover lines" when they read queries—in other words, how would this piece be described in a short headline on the magazine's cover? You should be thinking the same way.)

The third paragraph, what I call the "nuts and bolts" paragraph, includes a brief outline of what the story will look like. I'll mention the angle, suggested word count, and possible sources like experts and "real people" I plan to interview. I'll also pitch related sidebars, boxes, or accompanying pieces like quizzes to round out the main story. I almost always include a working title and suggest an appropriate section of the magazine for the story if I can. (For example, "Are you interested in this topic for your 'Women's Health' department?") This makes it clear that I've read the magazine and am familiar with it. Or I'll mention a recent story from the magazine to let the editor know I've looked at back issues. This certainly doesn't hurt; in fact it helps set your query apart from the dozens or even hundreds of queries she's wading through every month.

Finally, the fourth paragraph is what I call the "I-am-so-great" paragraph. This is where I highlight my writing experience and any relevant background information to demonstrate that I'm "uniquely qualified" to write the article. Are you pitching a parenting story? Then mention that you're a stay-at-home mom of four children. Do you want to write about using the Web for publicity? Include a sentence about your public relations background.

New writers often ask me if they should mention that they haven't been published yet. Well, the fact that you don't have clips (published copies of your work) may not be a reflection of your writing ability. Still, you needn't advertise that fact in your query either. In other words, avoid language like, "Although I have never published anything . . ." or "While I have been writing for years, no one seems to want to buy my work . . ." That's a definite turnoff.

Instead, highlight the writing experience you do have and your unique qualifications. Include a brief overview of your

Blow Your Own Horn

Spend as much time marketing yourself as you spend writing.

You should be searching the writing job boards for freelance gigs, contacting editors, reading up about news and changes in the magazine industry, and researching and writing queries.

Don't think that just because you're busy now you don't need to market yourself.

Keeping on top of new markets and job openings will help you keep an even flow of assignments coming in the door.

—Linda Formichelli, Blackstone, Massachusetts

general writing background (for example, writing for newsletters, newspapers, or local publications). And remember that your most important writing sample is the query itself.

While there is no magic formula to query-writing, your letter should capture the editor's interest, explain why readers will want to read the piece, describe how you plan to approach the subject, and convince the editor that you're the person for the assignment.

Writing queries is a skill, and the more you do, the better you become at it. Let's look at two actual queries that I sent out to two fitness magazines a few years ago.

The queries appear on the following two pages. Although at first glance they appear similar, they had very differing results.

February 14, 1997

Jennifer Cook
Executive Editor
Fitness
110 5th Avenue
New York, New York 10011

Dear Ms. Cook:

Most pregnant women are afraid that after the baby, their bodies will never be the same. They dread losing the fitness they have worked so hard to achieve, but they don't want to risk their babies' health to keep up their workouts.

Most obstetricians agree that regular moderate exercise is beneficial to pregnant women as long as they were in good physical condition before pregnancy. However, mothers-to-be are advised to exercise at or below a certain heart rate to protect the baby's safety. Using a heart monitor allows these women to keep up their fitness program and reassures them that their child is safe.

I am interested in writing a short article for *Fitness* on the use of heart rate monitors while exercising by pregnant women. I will interview mothers who successfully employed monitors through pregnancy and several physicians for their recommendations on exercise during pregnancy. This piece will also remind readers of the value of using heart monitors for working out even if they are not pregnant or planning on becoming so.

I am a freelance writer interested in health and fitness issues and have enclosed two recent clips for your review. Please call me at your convenience to discuss this idea further.

Thank you for your time. I look forward to hearing from you soon.

Very truly yours,
Kelly K. James

May 5, 1998

Ms. Megan McMorris
Senior Editor
Fit
1700 Broadway
New York, New York 10019

Dear Megan:

A recent study published in *The Lancet* tracked a competitive runner who continued to train throughout her pregnancy. To ensure the safety of her babies (she delivered healthy twins), she wore a heart rate monitor to maintain a heart rate of 130–140 beats per minute.

Heart rate training is growing in popularity, not just for pregnant women, but for time-crunched exercisers seeking ways to work out more efficiently and safely. Using a heart rate monitor can make cardiovascular training more effective as it helps ensure that athletes work out as intensely (or as easily) as they are supposed to. Starting at $100, a heart rate monitor is an inexpensive investment that can be worth much more for women looking to improve their fitness.

Interested in a story about the use of heart rate monitors to train more efficiently? "Target Your Training: How a Heart Rate Monitor Can Make You Fitter" will give an overview of how these monitors can be used to maximize training. I'll include advice from athletic trainers and female athletes who use monitors regularly about how to get the most from a heart monitor; a possible sidebar might include a list of some of the different models available. Although I estimate about 800 words for this story, that's flexible depending on your needs.

Interested in this story for your "exercise.sports.fitness" section or as a short feature? As you know, I've written for *Fit* before as well as for other magazines including *Cosmopolitan*, *Shape*, *Good Housekeeping*, *Modern Bride*, and *Bride's*.

I hope you'll find this story appropriate for a future issue of *Fit*; let me know if you have any questions about it. Thank you for your time; I look forward to hearing from you soon.

Very truly yours,
Kelly James-Enger

Both queries concern the same basic subject—using heart rate monitors. Yet the former was rejected (what I call "bonged") and the second was assigned. Why? While the first query isn't terrible, it isn't going to excite an editor either, for the following reasons:

- *It's much too general.* My lead starts out with an assumption that nearly anyone could make—that "most women" are afraid that pregnancy will irrevocably change their bodies. Then in the second paragraph, I make the sweeping assertion that "most obstetricians" say that "moderate exercise" is beneficial as long as women keep their heart rate at or below a certain level. How about some specifics here?

- *It's inaccurate.* If I would have done any background research, I would have discovered that the American College of Obstetricians and Gynecologists had recently rescinded its blanket recommendation that pregnant women exercise at or below 140 beats per minute. (Instead, pregnant women are supposed to monitor their exertion levels and not push themselves too hard.) If this editor knows anything about prenatal fitness, she'll probably catch this oversight immediately.

- *Look at my third paragraph.* "I am interested in writing a short article . . ." Boring, isn't it? I could have spiced this up a little.

- *Perhaps most important of all, I've misread the market.* Think about it—how many women who read *Fitness* are pregnant or trying to become so? I'd guess less than 5 percent. Yet this query is directed at that tiny subgroup, although I do mention that the piece "will also remind readers of the value of using heart monitors for working out even if they are not pregnant or planning on becoming so." If I was pitching a magazine like *Fit Pregnancy*, this wouldn't be an issue. But I'm pitching a general women's fitness magazine.

- *Finally, my "I-am-so-great" paragraph is not so great.* Although I mention my interest in health and fitness, I don't do a very good job of convincing the editor of my qualifications to write the article, do I?

Now look again at my second query. Much better, isn't it?

- *First, my lead includes a double whammy.* The mention of the recent study gives me both a time peg and evidence of a trend. *The Lancet* is a major British medical journal (along the lines of *The Journal of the American Medical Association* or *The New England Journal of Medicine*). I don't have to explain what it is because my editor works at a fitness magazine; otherwise, I'd include the phrase "a British medical journal."

- *In the second paragraph, I target the audience much more effectively.* While the study in question involved a pregnant woman, I immediately explain that heart rate monitors are growing in popularity, "not just for pregnant women, but for time-crunched exercisers seeking ways to work out more efficiently and safely." Aha! That's pretty much everyone who reads *Fit*, isn't it? Note that I also mention the benefits of using heart rate monitors and point out their affordability. A heart rate monitor costs only about $100—most readers would be able to purchase one. That's another selling point for this story.

- *In the third paragraph, I've tried to make the editor's job easy.* I've come up with a working title which is a little long but gives an idea of what the piece will look like; I've told her the type of sources I plan to interview; and I've suggested an appropriate, service-oriented sidebar. I go on to estimate word count, and then let her know that I've read the magazine by suggesting the department ("exercise.sports.fitness") the story seems right for. I also briefly mention my writing background; since I had worked with her before, I don't enclose clips.

- *But guess what?* My "I-am-so-great" paragraph is still weak. Why? At the time, I'd been using a heart rate monitor during runs for several years—a fact that certainly makes me "uniquely qualified" to write about them. But it slipped my mind to mention it in the query, although I wound up using my experience as a first-person lead in the story itself. Moral of the story: Nearly every query, no matter how good, can always be improved upon. And the more queries you write, the better they'll get.

On the following two pages, you'll see another example of a "before" and "after" query:

October 13, 1998
VIA FACSIMILE 1-212-767-5600

Ms. Madonna Behen
Health, Nutrition and Fitness Editor
Woman's Day

Dear Ms. Behen:

I'm writing to follow up on our recent phone conversation.

Kim, 33, had been working for a small insurance company for about six months when the fatigue began. She felt exhausted all the time, and was so drowsy driving home that she worried about falling asleep during her hour-long commute. She began going to bed earlier and earlier to catch up on her sleep, but the tiredness continued. Finally in frustration she consulted her doctor, who diagnosed her with sleep apnea.

Sleep apnea is just one of several medical conditions that continual fatigue can signal. Lingering fatigue that lasts for more than two weeks can also indicate a thyroid problem, chronic fatigue syndrome, depression, or anemia as well as other, more serious diseases. But how can you tell whether your tiredness suggests a medical problem—or is simply the result of a time-crunched schedule?

"Tired All the Time? What Your Fatigue May Mean" will examine the most common causes of fatigue and some of the more common disorders that it can signal. I'll include information and advice from respected medical professionals on the foregoing disorders; a possible sidebar might include tips on how to get better-quality sleep (since our schedules usually prevent us from getting as much sleep as we need!). Although I estimate a length of about 1,200 words for this story, that's flexible depending on your needs.

Interested in this story for your "Health" department? As you know, I'm a full-time freelancer who's written for *Cosmopolitan*, *Good Housekeeping*, *Complete Woman*, *Bride's*, *Bridal Guide*, *Vegetarian Times*, *Fit*, *Fitness*, and *American Woman*; let me know if you'd like additional clips to review. Please call me if you have questions about this story idea.

Thank you for your time; I look forward to hearing from you soon.

Very truly yours,
Kelly James-Enger

December 4, 1998
VIA FACSIMILE 1-212-767-5600

Ms. Madonna Behen
Health, Nutrition and Fitness Editor
Woman's Day

Dear Donna:

Nice speaking with you on Wednesday. Here's my revised query per our discussion:

How often do you run out of energy before you run out of day? Women—who juggle family, career and personal responsibilities every day—suffer from fatigue more often than men do. In fact, a study conducted earlier this year found that more than a quarter of women listed "persistent fatigue"—defined as a "sustained sense of exhaustion for at least six months"—as their number one health complaint. Eighty percent included fatigue in their "top ten" health concerns. Fortunately, you don't have to feel tired all the time—eating better, getting regular exercise, using relaxation techniques, and even changing your breathing are just some of the ways that your readers can use to reduce fatigue.

"Tired of Being Tired? Fatigue-Fighting Techniques" will describe proven ways of combating this common condition. I'll include advice from respected medical experts including Dr. David Bell, author of *Curing Fatigue,* and Dr. Ronald Hoffman, author of *Tired All the Time: How to Regain Your Lost Energy* as well as other nationally known physicians and researchers. One sidebar will describe some of the common disorders that persistent fatigue may signal (such as sleep apnea, thyroid problems, depression, and anemia); another will list some "fatigue-fighting" foods. Although I estimate a length of about 1,800 words for this story, that's flexible depending on your needs.

Interested in this story for your "Health" department? As you know, I'm a full-time freelancer who has written for *Good Housekeeping, Cosmopolitan, McCall's, Fitness, Fit, Shape, Bride's, Bridal Guide, Vegetarian Times,* and *Correspondent;* let me know if you'd like additional clips to review. Please call me if you have questions about this story idea.

Thank you for your time; I look forward to hearing from you soon.

Very truly yours,
Kelly James-Enger

In this case, I'd been pitching to *Woman's Day* for nearly a year. While I'd gotten close with a couple of ideas, nothing had quite hit the mark yet.

Health editor Donna Behen called to tell me that while she liked the idea of writing about women and fatigue, she thought more women were tired due to lifestyle and environmental factors (i.e., lack of sleep, poor nutrition, and lack of exercise) than because of medical reasons. She told me that she'd prefer that the main story address those issues, and to include the possible medical causes in a separate sidebar. (Again, think of the audience and pitch the story to appeal to as many readers as possible.)

I took her advice, rewrote the query, and sold the piece. Once again, my lead in the successful version does double-duty—it includes a recent survey (for timeliness) that also proves how prevalent fatigue is among women.

I go on to list some of the techniques that women can use to battle fatigue and suggest the type of experts I'll interview (physicians and researchers with a background in this area). The two sidebars were a direct result of my conversation with Donna. And finally, even though she knows who I am, I include a list of my publishing credits to convince other editors at *Woman's Day* that I'm qualified to write the piece.

One of the benefits of specializing is that you spend less time writing queries—I've even been known to use very similar queries to pitch an idea to different markets. While I would never do this with competing magazines (i.e., pitch the same idea to *Woman's Day* and *Family Circle*, or to *Bridal Guide* and *Wedding Bells*), I will if the markets are in different areas.

Consider these two queries:

June 30, 2000

Ms. Kate Lawler
Articles Editor
Parents
375 Lexington Avenue
New York, New York 10017

Dear Ms. Lawler:

Sharon Cindrich, 32, is mom to a five-year-old daughter and three-year-old son. While she and her husband haven't completely ruled out the idea of another baby, for now they're happy with the size of their family. During a routine doctor's visit, Sharon asked about birth control and was surprised when her doctor suggested she consider an IUD as a contraceptive option. She, like many women, believed that they had been taken off the market a long time ago.

Even savvy moms like Sharon aren't necessarily up-to-date on birth control issues. Do you know what emergency contraception is—and how to obtain it? What's the difference between birth control pills and mini-pills? Why shouldn't you use Depo-Provera if you want to become pregnant soon?

If you can't answer these questions, it may be time for a birth control brush-up. With more than 30 different brands of oral contraceptives currently on the market and new methods like the contraceptive patch being developed, women need to be aware of all available options so they can make informed choices about birth control. (The answers to the above questions: emergency contraception is available by prescription and, if used within 72 hours of intercourse, is 75 percent effective in preventing pregnancy; birth control pills contain both estrogen and progestin components while mini-pills contain only progestin; and Depo-Provera can remain effective for up to seven months after it is injected.)

"The Mom's Guide to Birth Control: Making the Best Choice" will look at the host of contraceptive options available, discuss their advantages and drawbacks, and help readers choose the best option for their current lifestyles. I anticipate a "Q and A" format but can structure the piece differently depending on your needs. I plan to interview nationally known physicians such as Dr. Gerson Weiss, chairman of the Obstetrics/Gynecology and Women's Health Department at the New Jersey Medical School, for this story. Possible sidebars might include comparisons of the effectiveness and cost of different birth control methods. (While you ran a short piece in "Adult Health & Fitness" on new contraceptive methods in the January 2000 issue, this feature will be an in-depth treatment of this important topic.) I estimate 1,500 words for this story, but that's flexible depending on your editorial needs.

Interested in this story for your "Health & Safety" section? I'm a full-time freelancer who has written for magazines including *Family Circle*, *Woman's Day*, *Marie Claire*, *Fitness*, and *Shape*; clips are enclosed. If you have any questions about this story idea, please let me know. Thank you for your time; I look forward to hearing from you soon.

Very truly yours,
Kelly James-Enger

January 31, 2001   [sent via e-mail]

Ms. Patricia Canole
Editor-in-Chief
For the Bride by Demetrios

Dear Pat:

Quick—take a minute from your wedding plans and answer the following questions:

Do you know what emergency contraception is—and how to obtain it? What's the difference between birth control pills and mini-pills? Why shouldn't you use Depo-Provera if you want to become pregnant soon?

If you can't answer these questions, it may be time for a birth control brush-up. With more than 30 different brands of oral contraceptives currently on the market and new methods like the contraceptive patch being developed, women need to be aware of all available options so they can make informed choices about birth control. (The answers to the above questions: emergency contraception is available by prescription and, if used within 72 hours of intercourse, is 75 percent effective in preventing pregnancy; birth control pills contain both estrogen and progestin components while mini-pills contain only progestin; and Depo-Provera can remain effective for up to seven months after it is injected.)

"The Bride's Guide to Birth Control: What You Need to Know" will look at the host of contraceptive options available, discuss their advantages and drawbacks, and help readers choose the best option for their current lifestyles. I anticipate a "Q and A" format but can structure the piece differently depending on your needs. I plan to interview nationally known physicians such as Dr. Gerson Weiss, chairman of the Obstetrics/Gynecology and Women's Health Department at the New Jersey Medical School, for this story. Possible sidebars might include comparisons of the effectiveness and cost of different birth control methods. I estimate 1,500 words for this story, but that's flexible depending on your editorial needs.

Pat, let me know if you want me to cover contraception in the next issue of *For the Bride* or if you have other story ideas you'd like me to write.

Thanks and have a great day!

Best,

Kelly

A couple of notes about these two queries:

- *First, there's practically no chance of overlapping markets.* Very few readers are going to be reading both *For the Bride by Demetrios* and *Parents.* Even if both stories are assigned (and they were), I'll write two completely different articles, using different experts, different quotes, and a different format. The basic subject matter—birth control—is the same, but the angle and the approach will be (and was) quite different.

- *Although the bodies of the queries are very similar, the leads reflect the readership of each magazine.* I'm "targeting the market" with each query. Brides and moms have different contraceptive issues and concerns, and I'm letting each editor know that I realize that.

- *Finally, notice the slight difference in tone.* I hadn't written for *Parents* before, so I sent a formal query with clips. (Note that I've let the editor know I looked at her magazine by mentioning a story she ran six months prior to my query!) I also give her the rundown on my writing experience. The query to *For the Bride* is less formal because I'd had a long-standing relationship with my editor there, and in fact was a contributing editor at the magazine by this point. She doesn't need to be reminded of my writing background—she just needs to see the query itself.

By the way, these are by no means my only stories on birth control. In the past several years, I've also written about:

- Emergency contraception for *Fit.*

- Oral contraceptives for *Marie Claire.*

- New developments in birth control for *Shape.*

- Health benefits of taking the pill continuously for *Redbook.*

- Fitness and health benefits of taking the pill continuously for *Oxygen.*

- The latest in birth control options for *Complete Woman.*

- Choosing the right contraception for *Complete Woman* (same topic, same market, but different angle and approach).

Because of accumulated knowledge, though, each query and resulting article takes far less time to research and write than if I was learning about a new subject every time. Remember, that's one of the positive features of specializing!

Gathering Facts: Places to Begin Your Research

As a freelancer, you should already be familiar with basic research techniques, so I won't spend too much time on them here. The Appendix lists a number of books that cover the how-tos of researching.

One great tip you may not find in those books: Become friends with the reference librarians at your local library. They've been invaluable when I've had trouble tracking down a specific piece of information or an obscure study. While I never expect them to do my job for me, I'll call and explain the steps I've taken and ask if they have any suggestions—and they often do. (Special kudos to the reference librarians at the Downers Grove Public Library, who are wonderful.)

In the following chapters of this book, which deal in more depth with different specialties, you'll find a number of resources, associations, governmental agencies, and other sources of information and experts specific to those areas. When it comes to finding experts in nearly any area, good starting points almost always include the following:

- *www.profnet.com and other on-line databases.* Profnet can be used in two ways. You can search its database of experts. Or you can submit a query specifying what type of expertise you're looking for, and their staff will send your request out to universities, hospitals, PR firms, and the like. I have had good luck with Profnet and use it occasionally. The downside of using it and similar databases is that you can be inundated with PR people who insist that their clients are the perfect sources for your story when in fact they are not. My advice: If you use it, opt for responses via e-mail rather than phone—it's easier and less time-consuming to turn people down who don't fit the bill with a quick e-mail note.

- *Encyclopedia of Associations.* This three-volume set should be on reserve at your local library. Thousands of organizations, associations, clubs, and other groups are listed, arranged by subject category. The encyclopedia lists organizations as varied as the American College of Sports Medicine and Man-watchers International. It's an excellent place to start your expert hunt. For example, if I'm writing a nutrition story, I can call the American Dietetic Association and ask for the names of some of their spokespeople. Whenever I'm writing about a particular subject area, I'll often check the encyclopedia to see if there's an association related to it—it's often a good place for background information as well. Then I call that association, ask for their public affairs or public relations department, and request a referral to a member of that group whom I can then interview. The PR person will know who the media-friendly members are and often will have background information on them as well—it's a huge time-saver.

- *Books on the subject.* Consider this the no-frills method of finding experts. If you can locate a book on a given subject—particularly one that's been published recently—the author is almost always happy to talk to you in exchange for getting the name of his book mentioned in the article. (Haven't you ever wondered why so many "experts" in magazine articles also happen to be authors? Now you know.) If your expert is a book author, you can often locate him through his publisher as well. Call the publisher and ask for the publicist who handles the book you're inquiring about; he or she can put you in touch with the author.

- *Universities/colleges.* Call their PR or public affairs office and ask for a referral to a professor or researcher in the area you're writing about. Also ask to be put on their press list for news releases and the like. (One note—the bigger and more well-respected the school, the better. You don't have to use Yale and Harvard every time, but you probably don't want to quote experts from Dr. Mike's School of Foot Doctors either.)

- *Other magazine stories.* If you've come across articles on the same or a similar subject and they quote intelligent-sounding experts, track them down to set up interviews. I've used a variety of Web-based search engines like www.google.com and Internet directories to find experts.

- *Family, friends, coworkers, neighbors, etc.* In other words, talk to everyone you can think of. When I'm writing a story and looking for "real people" anecdotes, I'm shameless. I'll hit up people at the gym, at the library, and even at Starbucks. (What can I say? Sometimes it helps to be an extrovert.) Create a network with your fellow writers so that you help each other out with story sources—the more geographically far-flung, the better. This is another benefit of using e-mail—you can hit up all your writer friends simultaneously, asking if they know any newlyweds, for example, with one quick note.

The Art of Interviewing: Some Tips

And it is an art. Although I'd conducted hundreds of depositions and interviews as a lawyer, interviewing a person as a journalist

Track Your Contacts

Using contact-management software and a Web site to market myself are key.

I am not a "salesman" type of guy at all. But treating every contact I make in the writing field as if it were a sales opportunity—and then entering that into my database—makes all the difference.

This is especially true when an editor says, "Call me back in two months."

I enter that into my database, and then I forget about it . . . until my computer reminds me two months later.

Even if the editor is blowing you off initially, he or she is usually impressed that you did what s/he asked and you said you would do.

—Ari Tye Radetsky, Denver, Colorado

is very different. I learned that I sometimes had to stop myself from asking leading questions, for example. But I learned quickly. And over the years, I've done interviews with hundreds of physicians, nutritionists, researchers, business experts, fitness professionals, and "real people."

I nearly always follow the same basic format when setting up an interview. I call and introduce myself, describe the story I'm writing, and ask the person if he or she is available for a brief telephone interview in the near future. (Once in a great while, I will conduct interviews in person or by e-mail, but 95 percent of the time, they're done by phone.) Unless I have an exceptionally short deadline, the first call is simply to arrange a convenient time to talk. This gives your source some time to think about the story, gather any necessary information, and prepare to speak with you.

A few interviewing tips:

- *When you call to conduct the interview, always ask first, "Is this still a good time for you to talk?"* Roughly a quarter of the time, the person will ask if I can call back so that he or she can attend to something else. That's fine with me—I want a source who isn't distracted by a crying child, encroaching deadline, or the need to run to the bathroom. Remember, they're doing you the favor, so accommodate their schedules.

- *At the outset, ask permission to tape-record the interview.* State laws vary, and you don't want to run into trouble with any wiretapping laws. Only twice have people refused to be taped; both were high-profile businessmen who had probably been burned by a taped comment in the past. Also, ask for the person's name and correct spelling; job title; name, date, and publisher of any relevant books; educational degrees and research areas (if appropriate); mailing address; e-mail address; and other contact information. (By the way, also ask how often the source checks his e-mail—some people like me check it constantly; others may only log on once or twice a week. If you're on deadline and need a quick question answered, e-mail may save you some time. But if the person rarely checks it, a phone call may be faster.)

- *Jot down the questions that you want to cover.* And keep them by the phone so you don't forget any. Ask general, open-ended questions and try to avoid ones that can be answered with a flat "yes" or "no." If I run into a particularly recalcitrant subject, I'll ask lots of "why" and "how" questions—like "Why did the results of your study surprise you?" or "How can this affect people's lives?" You want the interviewee to do the talking. Don't put words in his mouth.

- *Be patient and don't interrupt.* If a source is getting waaaaaay off target (you might think he would hear over the phone that my fingers are no longer typing furiously), I usually let him ramble on until he finishes his thought. Then I'll say something like, "Oh, that's interesting. Now, getting back to your current work . . ." and reel him back in.

- *At the end of the interview, ask if the person wants to add anything that you haven't thought to ask about.* You can also inquire if your source knows of anyone else you might talk to for the story—I've gotten great leads that way. I usually wrap up by saying something like, "Thank you so much for your time. I think I've got everything I need, but as I put the story together, I may run into a quick question, or my editor may ask for some information, that I didn't anticipate. Are you going to be around during the coming weeks, or do you have travel plans coming up? Also, do you prefer that I call or e-mail you with any additional questions?" This gives them the heads-up that I may be in touch in the future—and prevents me from looking stupid when I come back with a follow-up question.

- *Finally, I always send a personal thank you note.* Many writers don't, but I like to express my appreciation for the person's time. (Granted, I don't work for a daily newspaper, either, where writing thank you notes to dozens of people might seriously impact my productivity.) With the note, I include my business card and let the source know that I'll be in touch when the article is published so he or she can find it on the newsstand. (If it's a small-circulation magazine or a trade publication, I'll usually offer to send a photocopy of the story—not the magazine itself—to the source.) Yes, this takes some extra time and money, but your sources will appreciate it and remember you the next time you need an interview.

Always treat your sources well, and your job as a freelancer becomes much easier.

CHAPTER 4

A Case Study

An Article from Start to Finish

NONWRITERS OFTEN DON'T UNDERSTAND the amount of time and work that goes into an article, even (or especially!) shorter pieces. The time span between the initial query to publication can easily last six or nine months, often longer. And this assumes a fairly speedy reply to the query.

My personal record is an incredible 26 months between mailing a query and getting the phone call assigning the story. During that time, I'd married, changed my name, and changed careers. I was surprised that the editor was able to track me down!

To follow the lifecycle of an article, I'll use as an example one of the first fitness pieces I wrote. As you will see, I chose to pitch an article about relocating—with a fitness perspective—and queried *Shape*.

My initial query appears on the following page.

March 17, 1997

Ms. Peg Moline
Editorial Director
Shape
Weider Health & Fitness
21100 Erwin Street
Woodland Hills, California 91367

Dear Ms. Moline:

When Abby moved from Atlanta to Minneapolis, she was in for a shock. Living in the South, she had enjoyed bicycling, hiking, and rock climbing all year long. Minneapolis meant bitterly cold winters where outdoor exercise was out of the question, and after a few months she found herself feeling out of shape and depressed. It didn't help that she didn't know anyone in town except the people she worked with.

One year later, Abby's back in the fitness swing. She still hikes and bikes during the summer months and has learned to roller-blade. In the winter, she stays in shape with exercise videos and indoor roller-blading. She's also in a basketball league, and this winter is taking tap dance lessons. While she isn't crazy about the −50 degree wind chill, she enjoys the indoor sports and has made a lot of new friends from them, too.

Although the readers of *Shape* make health and fitness a priority, moving to a new city, a new state, or even just across town often disrupts a woman's exercise routine—but it can also be the opportunity to break out of a fitness rut.

I am interested in writing a short article for your magazine on how to survive a move to a new place. The piece will include anecdotes such as the above and will include advice on how to make the transition easier. This short, helpful article might appear in "Rut Buster" or "Inner Shape" or could be run as a short feature. As a freelance writer (who has survived four moves in four years) and exercise buff, I believe I can bring a unique perspective to this topic. I am familiar with the tone and format of your magazine and have enclosed two recent clips for your review.

Thank you for your time. I look forward to hearing from you soon.

Very truly yours,
Kelly K. James

Having heard nothing, I then sent this follow-up letter (below) a few months later.

Little did I know, as a new freelance writer, that the time span between when I first pitched the idea and then eventually saw the finished article in print would be 19 months.

As I've discovered, having the ability and persistence to navigate a steady course following an article from start to completion—to track queries, follow-up as needed, and finally make sure the finished article fits what that particular editor needs—is one of the important skills of a successful freelancer.

[follow-up letter]

June 11, 1997

Ms. Peg Moline
Editorial Director
Shape
Weider Health & Fitness
21100 Erwin Street
Woodland Hills, California 91367

Dear Ms. Moline:

I write to follow up on my query about moving, which I submitted to you in March. Since I haven't had a response from you yet, I've taken the liberty of enclosing a copy of that letter for your convenience.

If you have any questions, please give me a call. If I don't hear from you in another six weeks or so, I'll assume you can't use this idea at the moment and may market it elsewhere.

Thank you for your time and consideration. I look forward to hearing from you soon.

Very truly yours,
Kelly James-Enger

Here's a look, then, at the specific steps taken—and the time involved—to write this seemingly straightforward 600-word fitness story:

1. *Come up with the idea.* This was an easy one. I'd moved several times in the previous years. For me, part of the fun of living in a new city was finding running routes and exploring my new home on foot. When one of my friends relocated from sunny Atlanta back to the Twin Cities, I had the perfect lead for my query . . . which I used.

2. *Find an appropriate market.* As usual, I started with *Writer's Market* and *The Writer's Handbook*, looking at the guidelines for women's fitness magazines. *Shape, Fitness, Fit,* and *Self* all seemed like possibilities—but *Shape* had a column called "Rut Buster" that I thought the idea was perfect for . . . so I pitched the story there first.

3. *Write the query.* The query didn't take me too long to write. It's an okay query, but not spectacular—I could have done a better job of fleshing out the idea. My "I-am-so-great" paragraph is pretty good though—who better to write this piece than me?

4. *Follow up.* I didn't hear from the editor, so I sent a follow-up letter in June, asking if she was interested in the story idea.

5. *Phone call/assignment.* In November, Suzanne Schlossberg, an editor at *Shape,* called to assign the piece. We discussed the length (600 words), the pay ($1.20/word for all rights), the deadline, and possible sources for the piece. (Note: Now that I am farther along in my career, I usually don't sign all-rights contracts because they prevent me from selling any reprint rights to the story in the future. But as a new free-lancer, I was more concerned with amassing clips and less concerned with the rights I was giving up.)

Suzanne wanted me to interview a sports psychologist as well as a ski instructor, who could comment on what to do—and not to do—when taking up a new sport. She had a pretty clear idea of what she wanted out of the story. Because I was a relatively new writer, she also asked me to write an outline of the piece before I started. (Because of my inexperience, she could have conceivably asked me to write "on spec" (on speculation), meaning that she'd be happy to read the finished piece but with no guarantee that she'd wind up buying it. While I did write a few pieces on spec when I was starting out, I wouldn't do it now.)

6. *Find my sources.* The next step was to find appropriate sources for the story. My friend Abby was my first call. I gave her a buzz and told her I'd be interviewing her for the story. I then called the American Running Association at (800) 776-2732 and asked if the public affairs person there could suggest a qualified sports psychologist. She recommended Jack Lesyk, Ph.D., director of the Ohio Center for Sport Psychology. To locate a ski instructor, I simply put in the words "Jackson Hole ski instruction" in www.altavista.com and found a number of ski schools. I called one, asked for an extroverted instructor who wouldn't mind being interviewed, and got Jamie Mackintosh's name and number. I called all of my sources and lined up the interviews.

7. *Draft rough outline.* Per Suzanne's request, I wrote an outline of the piece and e-mailed it to her for her approval; she said it looked fine. While submitting an outline does take additional time, it ensures that you and your editor are on the same page as far as the story goes.

8. *Prepare for/conduct interviews.* Using my outline as a guide, I made a short list of questions to ask my sources. I conducted all three interviews by phone and then transcribed my notes. I also sent personal thank you notes to Abby, Jack, and Jamie,

and told them I'd be in touch with any follow-up questions or to let them know when the story was published.

9. *Write first draft.* After reading through my interview notes, I wrote my first draft. I used a first-person lead, at Suzanne's suggestion. (During our phone conversations, I'd mentioned that when I moved to St. Louis, I also signed up for a marathon training group and ran my first marathon. She thought this was a great way to start the story. Well, duh. Why didn't I think of that when I was writing the query?)

10. *Edit/finalize draft.* Not surprisingly, my original draft was too long. So I then went back through the piece and pared it down to close to 600 words. I set it aside for a day or so and then came back to finish the final draft—reading through it word by word until I was satisfied that it was perfect, or at least as close as I would get. I turned it in to Suzanne the day before deadline, in December 1997. (Oh, by the way—turn in stories a day or two early and editors will remember you. Why? Because most writers turn in their work the day it's due—or later.)

11. *Phone call from Suzanne.* Suzanne said I had a great start to the story, but had some suggestions. She wanted me to tighten the lead and to get stronger quotes from Jack and Abby. I made notes of her suggestions, and we agreed to a deadline for the revision.

12. *Revise story.* I called Jack and Abby back, obtained additional quotes, and revised the story per Suzanne's suggestions. I turned in the piece in January 1998, then waited . . .

13. *Good news!* Suzanne calls to tell me the piece has been accepted. She asks me to turn in my fact-checking material (in this case, the names and telephone numbers of everyone I interviewed) and says that she's "putting payment through"—meaning I should see my check soon. (Some

magazines want you to provide them with an invoice, while others don't. Don't forget to ask your editor whether you need to send one.)

14. *Get paid!* Woo hoo! The check arrives sometime in February . . . and I happily cash it. Then I wait to see the piece in print.

15. *Get published!* Alas, the story doesn't run in June as originally anticipated. But it finally appears in the October 1998 issue. I call my sources to let them know the date of the issue and the page the story starts on, leaving my phone number in case they have any questions. A full 19 months after my initial query, I see the bylined article in the magazine.

On the pages that follow, you'll find my original story, and the revised version. I think Suzanne's suggestions made for a stronger piece—that's the benefit of working with a good editor.

While some writers tend to be protective (sometimes overly protective, in my opinion) of their words, I'm usually not that sensitive if an editor wants to tweak a lead or reorganize a piece—it often makes the story better.

However, there have been several occasions when I turned in a story only to have it so badly mangled that I barely recognized it when it ran. Was I happy about it? No, but when it comes to a standoff between you and the editor, your editor will nearly always win. Choose your battles, and never let an argument over your story become personal.

[Here's my article as originally submitted.]

Kelly James-Enger   617 words
1312 DuPont Avenue #D   Rights per contract
Morris, IL 60450
(815) 942-8521
kjames@matrix.uti.com

Get a Move On:
Relocating Can Jump-Start Your Fitness Routine

When I was 25, I graduated from law school and moved to St. Louis from a small town for my first "real" job. I was miserable the first couple of months—I'd never lived in a large city before, I knew only two people in town, and going from the laid-back lifestyle of a student to 60-hour workweeks was a shock. The only constant in my life was my running—my morning runs helped me get to know my neighborhood and cope with the pressures of my new career. I even found that living in a big city had advantages—I joined a marathon-training program that revitalized my training and helped me successfully complete my first marathon that fall. Participating in the program also helped me meet dozens of other local runners at our Sunday morning runs and eventually make friends in my new location.

Relocating—whether it's across town or across the country—is often the perfect time to reevaluate your exercise program. "Relocating can be an opportunity to breathe some new life into your fitness routine," says Jack J. Lesyk, sports psychologist and Director of the Ohio Center for Sport Psychology in Beachwood, Ohio. Lesyk suggests looking at your current workout program and asking yourself what you really enjoy and whether you'd benefit from a change. "Maybe you've gotten a little tired of doing indoor machine workouts and you can now try some different outdoor activities," he says.

Moving from one climate to another may force you to change your exercise strategy. My friend Abby biked, hiked, and rock-climbed year-round when she lived in Atlanta, but now lives in Minneapolis. Although she still bikes during the summer, she's found creative ways to maintain her fitness during the cold Minnesotan winters—she roller-blades indoors, plays basketball at the Y, and takes tap and ballet classes.

72   *Ready, Aim, Specialize!*

No matter how busy you are during those first few months in a new place, make time for working out. "Exercising can help you maintain a 'centeredness' when other things are changing," says Leysk. "Moving involves a lot of stress and changes, so you want to hang on to something familiar and comforting. It helps psychologically, not just physically."

Keeping fit can also help you break into your new community and meet new people who have similar interests. If you worked out at a gym before, make finding one a priority—and try to go at the same time of day so you'll begin to recognize people. Check the Yellow Pages for "health clubs" to see what your new city offers and if they have a running or biking club you can join—I've found this is another way to make friends right away.

If your move inspires you to try a new sport, make sure you know what you're doing before you start. "Taking lessons with a professional instructor will help you learn correct technique and progress much more quickly than if you try to learn on your own," says Jamie Mackintosh, a professional ski instructor and training coordinator at the Jackson Hole Ski School in Wyoming. Although being in good physical shape will help you master new sports, Mackintosh adds, "when you try something new, it's normal to be sore no matter how fit you are. Your body is adjusting to using the muscles in a different pattern."

Even the most well-organized move can disrupt your regular routine, but staying fit will help you handle the stress and make your transition less difficult. I should know—I've moved five times in the past six years, and running has helped me survive every one. Even better, it helps a new place feel more like home, no matter where I live.

-30-

[Here's the revised version.]

Kelly James-Enger
1312 DuPont Avenue #D
Morris, IL 60450
(815) 942-8521
kjames@matrix.uti.com

625 words
Rights per contract

Get a Move On:
Jump-Start Your Fitness Routine When You Relocate
by Kelly James-Enger

When I was 25, I made the biggest move of my life—from a small
college town to St. Louis for my first job as a lawyer. I'd never lived in
a big city before, I was working sixty hours a week, and I was lonely.
When I heard about a marathon-training program that fall, I figured
it would be a good way to meet people—and I'd always dreamt of running a marathon.

For the next three months, I spent Thursday evenings listening to
different experts give advice on training, nutrition, and stretching and
Sunday mornings doing long runs with fellow program participants.
By the end of November, I was in the best shape of my life—and completed my first marathon in 4:11.

Relocating—whether across town or across the country—is the
perfect time to add something different to your exercise mix. "Relocating can be an opportunity to breathe some new life into your fitness
routine," agrees Jack Lesyk, sports psychologist and Director of the
Ohio Center for Sport Psychology in Beachwood, Ohio. Why not try
a high-energy spinning class instead of step aerobics? Yoga may be the
perfect antidote to a weightlifting program that's become a bore, and
experimenting with new machines like the popular elliptical trainers
can bring back the excitement to your workouts.

Your move may even force you to change your routine. When
my friend Abby lived in Atlanta, she biked, hiked, and played tennis
and basketball year-round—until her company transferred her to
Minneapolis.

"I dreaded the Minnesota winters because I love to exercise outside," she says. "But some days it's 20 below here. You're not even supposed to be outside!" Still, she admits, Minneapolis has its perks. "I had

always wanted to learn to roller-blade, but Atlanta was too hilly. Now I roller-blade outdoors in the summer and at the Metrodome in the winter." She adds, "And I've taken tap and ballet classes, too—I'd never have done that before."

Trying something new can also motivate you to work out during this busy time. "Exercising can help you maintain a 'centeredness' when other things are changing," says Leysk. "Moving involves a lot of stress and changes, so you want to hang on to something familiar and comforting. It helps psychologically, not just physically."

If you're inspired to try a new sport, consider some initial instruction. "Taking lessons with a professional instructor will help you learn correct technique and progress much more quickly than if you try to learn on your own," says Jamie Mackintosh, a professional ski instructor and training coordinator at the Jackson Hole Ski School in Wyoming. And cut yourself some slack—even if you're an expert in one sport, it takes time to master a new one. "When you try something new, it's normal to be sore no matter how fit you are," says Mackintosh. "Your body is adjusting to using the muscles in a different pattern."

When you move to a new place, scope out what your community offers. Stop by the local bike or running store to ask about clubs and races, and check out area health clubs. (Look for a gym that offers a wide range of equipment and classes so you'll have plenty of options to choose from.) Community centers, park districts and recreation departments, and community colleges are also good places to inquire about fitness classes and activities.

Finally, don't forget that relocating is an adventure. I've moved four times in five years, and each move has boosted my training, encouraging me to set new goals with the promise of undiscovered running trails and a sense of starting over. A new home signals the beginning of a new chapter in your life. Make this one your best yet.

-30-

Building Relationships: The Key to Success

When it comes to nonfiction writing and marketing techniques for freelance writers, let me emphasize one more thing. When I started freelancing, my primary focus was to gain experience and create a portfolio of work.

What I've learned, however, is your real ticket to success as a freelancer—regardless of whether you specialize—isn't being able to pitch timely ideas, research topics, or turn in accurate, well-reported stories on deadline. Yes, those things certainly are essential. But the key is developing relationships with editors.

Think about it. You're far more likely to get an assignment from an editor you've worked with before (assuming you did a good job!) than from an editor who's completely new to you. Furthermore, as you build relationships, you'll also find that editors come to you with stories.

As a long-standing contributor, you'll also discover that you're in a good position to ask for—and get—higher rates for your work.

I've worked with many of the same editors for years, and I value my relationships with them. They know that I'm responsive, easy to work with, accurate, and that I never miss a deadline. And that helps ensure a continual flow of work.

Sure, there have been times when I've been disappointed with the way a story turned out or frustrated by an editor sitting on a story for months—and then killing it because "it just doesn't seem timely." (Um, well, it *was* when I turned it in five months ago!) But I never let an editor know my dissatisfaction. I might cross the person off my list, and not work for him or her again, but I don't burn bridges.

If I'm upset about something, I'll call another writer and commiserate. I won't take it out on the editor. I always strive to remember that I'm a self-employed business person first, a writer second.

Keep that in mind and act accordingly, regardless of what you write about. Smart writers understand that good businesses grow when relationships are built, respected, and maintained.

It's one of the most effective strategies you can use to create a successful, well-paying career as a freelance writer.

SECTION TWO

The Top Ten Hottest Specialties

CHAPTER 5

An Apple a Day

Writing About Health

The Basics: What You Need to Know

Nearly every periodical runs some sort of health-related stories, and for good reason—this topic affects us all regardless of sex, race, age, income, or profession. Parents want to know how to treat and prevent childhood diseases and ensure their kids' well-being. Women read up on gynecological issues like premenstrual syndrome, pregnancy and birth, and how to avoid diseases like breast and ovarian cancer. Baby boomers seek ways to lower their risk of disease and improve the quality of their lives.

Whether it's a newsy article on the latest developments in AIDS research, a straightforward piece on how to reduce your risk of heart disease, or a rundown of alternative therapies like magnets, aromatherapy, and herbal remedies, health writing is a continually growing and lucrative field. While it doesn't hurt to have a medical background to specialize in this area, the key to succeeding is being able to conduct accurate research. You must know where to locate information and be able to separate fact from fiction, speculation from science. You may also have to translate complicated medical concepts and jargon into language that readers can comprehend and, if appropriate, apply it to their lives.

The Nuts and Bolts: How to Write About Health

Accuracy Is Paramount

While editors and markets vary in terms of their approaches to health stories, there are a number of basic strategies to keep in mind when writing about this subject. The first and most important is the need to be both accurate and clear. Whether you're recommending that readers take a certain amount of vitamin C to reduce the risk of contracting a cold or describing how to perform a monthly breast exam, you must be able to write with specificity—while avoiding medical jargon or terms that the average reader won't understand.

Of course if you're writing for a more specialized audience such as a professional medical journal or a trade magazine aimed at physicians, this may be less of a concern. Many health writers have developed a background in their subject areas, but readers probably don't have the same level of expertise. When writing for a general audience, you may have to explain some basic concepts. When in doubt, let the market and your editor be your guides.

Be Timely

Much of health-based reporting is founded on newly published studies and the latest research. Health journalists must stay on top of breaking news and be able to pitch ideas that tie into the latest headlines; try to have a news peg in your health-related queries to convince the editor of the story's timeliness. For example, when the body mass index (BMI) was first introduced as the new standard of healthy weight in June 1998, dozens of articles were immediately published explaining what it was and how to calculate your own. Other articles questioned its usefulness and how this new standard would affect health care.

Has a new drug recently become available? Is a new fad diet sweeping the country? Find something timely about the story you're pitching and highlight it in your query. This will demonstrate your familiarity with this subject area and help you break in with new markets as well.

Get a Handle on Research

With tens of thousands of research articles published every year, there is no shortage of studies that can be tweaked into queries, cited in articles, or used to support your writing. Yet not all studies are created equal. In general, the larger the study, the better. Research on humans is more credible than studies conducted on rats, mice, or other animals. Most magazines will expect you to turn in copies of any research articles you refer to for fact-checking by them, so you can't fudge here. Make sure that you understand how the research was conducted—was it a controlled, clinical trial, for example, or simply a review article summarizing the published research—before you cite the results in a story.

Here are some factors to keep in mind when you review research studies:

• *Was the study randomized and double-blind?* In other words, were the researchers themselves unaware of which subjects comprised the control group and which were the experimental? Or was it a controlled study, meaning that the researchers sought to change only one variable out of many?

- *How many people were involved and over what period of time?* Usually, the greater the number of subjects involved and the longer a study lasts, the more weight it carries.

- *What were the demographics of the people involved?* Were both men and women included? What ages were they? How were they selected to participate in the study?

- *Was it an animal or human study?* The results of an animal study can suggest what may happen in humans, but usually isn't considered conclusive.

- *Who conducted and who sponsored the study?* Was the study conducted by a major university or hospital? Was it an independent study or was it underwritten in whole or in part by a corporation or association that may have a vested interest in the results of the research (for example, a bottled-water supplier supporting a study on how much water is needed for optimal health)?

- *Did the results confirm or agree with existing research or were the results surprising?* Why?

- *Does the study have significant health implications or consequences for people?* If so, for whom?

When writing about health, you simply can't take research at face value and should be leery about trumpeting its significance, says Margaret Littman, a freelancer based in Chicago who specializes in health and business topics.

"You have to be critical of any studies you read and any medical information you get. I find editors want someone who can question a doctor, question a medical expert, and question a study finding," says Littman. "Also, you definitely have to know the terminology, like was it a double-blind study or a study that was done on rats or on humans? In health writing, there are so many cases where there is a small study and it gets blown out of proportion and misreported as something that can apply to humans or apply in some ways that haven't been proven yet."

Consider the Audience

Writers should keep in mind that the majority of health writing is service-oriented. Why is someone reading this story? What will she gain by taking the time to finish it? How will it affect her life? While medical information can be dry, a good health writer is able to impart it in an entertaining or new way.

"You can't just quote the experts . . . you need to find some way to get readers to relate to the information, whether it's anecdotes or humor," says Littman. "Just because these are serious topics doesn't mean you have to be grave all the time. I don't think you can be, if you expect anyone to read things."

And while some topics are evergreen, successful health writers come up with new ways to pitch tried-and-true stories. "To a certain extent in health writing, more than in other categories, you can repeat the obvious," agrees Littman.

"People know that the way to lose weight is to exercise more and eat less, and people know the way not to get sick is to wash their hands, but there are no magic formulas. A lot of it is repeating the sensible advice whenever you're debunking whatever fad is not sensible."

Target Your Market

As with any article, your approach to a health story will depend on the markets you're pitching to. Do they run a lot of investigative articles? Is their focus on traditional medicine or alternative health? Do they prefer longer articles or shorter pieces with many sidebars?

Make sure that the idea and the angle you're pitching are targeted to that specific market. For example, a magazine aimed at young women probably won't be interested in a feature-length piece on osteoporosis. A parenting magazine might prefer articles about common children's health maladies like colds, ear infections, asthma, and bumps and bruises over rarer diseases. Make sure your angle and your approach is a good fit for the magazine before you send the query.

Research, Research, Research

As mentioned, the most critical aspect of writing about health is being able to accurately research and report stories. That may involve tracking down articles from obscure medical journals, interviewing physicians and researchers, and making sense of medical jargon.

First stop for any health reporter is the on-line library for the National Institute of Medicine, which currently has more than 11 million citations. Found at http://www.ncbi.nlm.nih.gov/PubMed/, it can be searched by keyword, author's name, date, and other parameters. The article citations give a brief description of the type of research involved and summarize the results; you can then access the articles on-line or request them through your local library. Many local libraries also carry issues of major medical journals like *The Journal of the American Medical Association* (JAMA) and *The New England Journal of Medicine*. Hospital and university libraries also have large selections of medical journals; check your local ones to see if they grant access to writers researching stories.

While the Internet has made researching health topics much easier, not all of the information you find on-line is accurate or even credible. However, there are a number of government health sites such as the ones for the Centers for Disease Control and Prevention (http://www.cdc.gov/), the National Institutes of Health (http://www.nih.gov/), and the National Center for Health Statistics (http://www.cdc.gov/nchs/default.htm) that every health writer should bookmark. If you find information on a site that you want to use, e-mail to confirm that it's accurate and the most recent data the organization or agency has; you can then turn in the response along with your fact-checking material when you turn in the story.

Finding the Experts

In the world of health writing, good experts are a must—and that usually means looking beyond your own internist or pediatrician. You'll need credentialed, recognized experts to back up any claims you make, and there are many ways to find them.

Professional associations such as the American Medical Association, the American College of Sports Medicine, and the American College of Obstetricians and Gynecologists all have public relations staffers who can suggest potential interviewees. Check out the *Encyclopedia of Associations*, a three-volume set that should be available at your local library—it includes thousands of listings for organizations, associations and groups.

You can also call the public affairs offices at major universities for recommendations. Or look for recent books on the subject and track down authors to request interviews. Call the publisher directly to ask if they will give you an author's contact information—explain that you're working on an article and might end up citing that person's book—or search the Web to find his or her contact info.

There are also a number of on-line databases that journalists can access to find experts. The largest and most popular is www.profnet.com, which can be used two ways. You can search the database of experts by using keywords. Or you can submit a query, detailing the type of story you're working on and the kind of expertise you're looking for. Profnet staffers will then send your request to academic, corporate, and public service sources who will contact you via phone or e-mail if they have possible leads.

Search Your Hard Drive

Every interview that I do is stored on my hard drive. Those are a potential gold mine for information. So I have to have a way to get to them.

Also, I sign up for a lot of technology and business newsletters, and get 10 to 15 e-mail newsletters and 25 to 40 press releases every day. I don't read all those, but I keep them on my hard drive in Microsoft Outlook for about six months. Then when I'm looking for information, I have programs like Enfish to search on keywords so I can pull up information.

I don't keep any paper— it's too hard and too messy, but with the computer I can keep things like press releases for six months and keep articles and transcripts forever.

—Sam Greengard, Burbank, California

Interviewing Experts

Interviewing a medical source isn't that different from interviewing anyone else. When calling someone to arrange an interview, introduce yourself and explain who you are, the nature of the story you're working on, and why you'd like to speak with the person. Is he considered an expert in the field? Has she conducted research that you want to include in the story? It doesn't hurt to flatter someone by saying, "I've read your book and think you'd be an excellent resource for this piece"—assuming it's true.

If the person is a doctor, ask if he or she is board-certified in any particular area; you'll also want to ask what areas an expert conducts his or her research in. Does he have a specialty? Is he affiliated with a pharmaceutical company or does he perform spokesperson work for an organization? This may affect the person's credibility and is something you need to know at the outset.

Try to keep your questions open-ended. Asking "how" and "why" is a good way to delve deeper when you get short answers. Don't interrupt—make sure that the person has finished each answer before you move on. You may find that some answers provoke questions that you hadn't considered, so pay attention to what the person is saying and follow up if necessary. If your source slips into medical jargon, ask her if she can explain what she's saying "to the average person" or "so readers will understand what you mean."

At the conclusion of the interview, review your list of questions and confirm that you've covered everything you wanted to. Ask your source if he'd like to add anything or comment further. You can also inquire as to whether he's aware of anyone else—another physician or researcher, for example—who might have relevant information as well. This is often an effective way of developing additional leads.

Avoid Absolute Certainty

Finally, remember that there are few absolutes when it comes to health writing. "I think in health, more than in any other writing, you need to qualify what you say," says Littman. "For example, you might write, 'This might help' or 'This may do this'—because nothing works for everyone. I think you have to be more cautious about the conclusions that you draw."

Keep in mind that physicians, researchers, and other experts will often disagree over even the most basic concepts, ranging from the causes of disease to preventive medicine. For example, one gynecologist may feel that the health benefits of taking oral contraceptives outweigh any possible dangers, while another thinks women should avoid taking the pill entirely.

Experts are entitled to their opinions, and those opinions will be influenced by their individual research areas, experiences, and beliefs. Particularly when you're writing about controversial areas, make sure that your articles address the current schools of thought. Your job as a health writer is to present a balanced picture of the information that is available—and let the reader judge for himself.

Tales from the Front: Linda Wasmer Andrews

Linda Wasmer Andrews started with a bachelor's degree in psychology and has been writing about health since the early 1980s. "I've covered everything from AIDS to zoonoses [diseases that can be spread from animals to people]," says Andrews, who lives in Albuquerque, New Mexico. "Recently, I've done a lot of writing about arthritis, diabetes, aging, depression, and stress. But I've also touched on nutrition, fitness, complementary/ alternative medicine, substance abuse, and a host of other topics."

Andrews' work has appeared in books, magazines, newsletters, and Web sites, and she has written for both consumers and health care professionals. She says she thinks of herself as a "generalist specialist" and says that one of the keys to her success is her sincere interest in and affinity for the subject. "The bottom line is that I genuinely believe I'm helping other people," says Andrews. "While 'careers' may get stale and boring, missions last.

"I get a lot of satisfaction from asking myself what other people really want and need to know about keeping their bodies and minds healthy, then going to experts to find the best answers. And then trying to communicate that information in a helpful, readable way."

She offers these tips to writers who want to specialize in health writing:

- *Take your job seriously.* This is people's health you're dealing with, so you have a solemn responsibility to seek out the most reliable, up-to-date information from the most authoritative sources.

- *Translate doctor-speak into plain English.* Talk about an ear infection, not "otitis media." Your readers are bright folks, but they may have neither the time nor the inclination to learn a whole new language.

- *Put news in perspective.* Science moves ahead in baby steps, not giant leaps. Every development is not necessarily revolutionary or a breakthrough, and there's no such thing as a miracle cure.

- *Place risks in a context your readers can relate to.* Offer meaningful comparisons of risks versus benefits, man-made risks versus natural ones, and unfamiliar risks versus more familiar ones.

- *Use solid statistics to back up your statements.* But avoid fuzzy phrases, such as "up to 10,000 cases," which could mean anywhere from 100 to 10,000 cases. It's better to say something that comes closer to the facts, such as "an estimated 9,000 cases."

- *Cite sound research evidence.* Tell your readers how large and well-controlled the study was, where it was conducted or published, and what the major implications and limitations of the data are.

Andrews reminds journalists to write about people, not diseases. "Don't define people by their diseases or medical status. Call a person with diabetes just that, not a diabetic or a patient," she says. "And remember that not everyone with a disease is automatically a 'victim' of it."

Finally, she also warns writers not to scare readers. "Of course, you want to tell the truth, even if it's grim, but you can do so tactfully. Talk about low survival rates rather than high death rates," adds Andrews. "And never leave your readers feeling helpless or hopeless. Give them practical action tips, and point them to helpful resources."

The Markets: Where to Sell Your Work

Health writing offers perhaps the broadest cross-section of markets of any specialty, and pay rates tend to be on the high side for consumer and many trade magazines.

Some of the biggest markets for health-related writing include:

- *General interest magazines*—cover varied topics including new medicine, scientific breakthroughs, preventive health, alternative medicine, health policy, and other related areas.

- *Professional and trade journals*—depending on the journal, may have a narrower range of interest; some journals cover only a limited subject area. There are trade journals aimed at specific practice areas such as dentistry, sports medicine, and obstetrics as well as more general ones that cover marketing, managing practices, and other business-related topics.

- *Women's and men's magazines*—cover a broad range of health-related subjects, mostly service-oriented. Women's magazines also include profile-type pieces about people who have faced medical challenges; both men's and women's magazines also cover diet and fitness topics as well. (See other chapters for more information about these specialties.)

- *Parenting magazines*—cover children's health, nutrition, development, childhood diseases, first aid, and preventive health. Some magazines also feature women's health articles, particularly those related to conception, pregnancy, and birth.

- *Health and fitness magazines*—similar to general interest magazines in terms of coverage; broad scope of nearly every health-related topic. These markets tend to be aimed at more specialized audiences, however—women in their 20s and 30s, for example, or men and women 50 and up—so keep that in mind when pitching stories.

- *Cooking/food magazines*—again, there's a good deal of cross-over between nutrition and health-related subjects. Many of these magazines will cover health topics, often focusing on preventive health.

- *Science magazines*—while they have a narrower range of interest, these markets often cover breakthroughs in medical technology or other new research findings.

- *Health-oriented Web sites*—these markets cover a variety of health topics. As in other on-line publications, stories tend to run shorter than in print markets and include quizzes, links to other sites, and other interactive features.

- *Specialty publications*—these markets are aimed at people who have a specific disease or condition like arthritis, diabetes, or cancer. More limited area of interest, but still cover a wide range of topics with an emphasis on service to readers.

- *National/major newspapers*—cover a wide range of health topics.

- *Regional/city magazines and newspapers*—like their national counterparts, regional and city publications also cover a broad range of health-related topics, many with a local angle.

In addition to markets looking for articles, there are a variety of other opportunities for writers who specialize in health, including freelancing for pharmaceutical companies, hospitals, and public relations agencies. Many writers also cover medical conferences and other events, or develop regular beats in particular areas of health and medicine.

Other Useful Stuff

As already mentioned, in the field of health, it's important to keep up on the newest developments. The more access you have to what's going on, the better. Sign up for e-mail news releases from sites like Reuters and newsdesk.com, which will update you on newly published studies and research. You can also register for e-mail lists and get on the press lists for medical organizations, colleges, and universities, which will notify you about breaking news.

Other potential sources of information include:

On-line Resources:

InteliHealth
www.intelihealth.com
Offers free e-mail newsletters on a variety of health-related topics; Web site also includes basic health information.

Newsdesk
www.prnmedia.com
Newsdesk also offers free e-mail newsletters on health care and health research.

Newswise
http://www.newswise.com
Newswise offers free e-mail newsletters on health; maintains press releases and an on-line directory of experts.

Profnet
www.profnet.com
Search the on-line database or submit a query to find experts in particular areas; you can also sign up for free e-mail releases about new research and story ideas.

PubMed
http://www.ncbi.nlm.nih.gov/PubMed/
PubMed provides on-line access to the National Library of Medicine.

Reuters Health
http://www.reutershealth.com/
Site that includes daily news releases about health, medicine, and nutrition.

Government Agencies

Centers for Disease Control and Prevention
Headquarters: 1600 Clifton Road, NE
Atlanta, GA 30333
Public inquiries: 404-639-3534
Washington office:
200 Independence Ave., SW
HHH Building, #746-G

Washington, D.C. 20201-0004
Phone: 202-690-8598
Fax: 202-690-7519
Web: www.cdc.gov
The CDC surveys worldwide disease trends, epidemics, and environmental health problems; maintains statistics; and promotes preventive health.

Health and Human Services Department
200 Independence Ave., SW, #615F
Washington, D.C. 20201
Phone: 202-690-7000, press inquiries 202-690-6343
Fax: 202-690-7203
Web: www.hhs.gov
HHS encompasses the Centers for Medicare and Medicaid Services, the Administration for Children and Families, the Public Health Service, and the Centers for Disease Control and Prevention.

National Center for Health Statistics
6525 Belcrast Road, #1140
Hyattsville, MD 20782
Phone: 301-458-4500, press inquiries 301-458-4800
Fax: 301-458-4020
Web: http://www.cdc.gov/nchs/default.htm
The NCHS compiles, analyzes, and disseminates national and international statistics on all matters pertaining to health.

National Institutes of Health
1 Center Dr., Building 1, #126
Bethesda, MD 20892-0148
Phone: 301-496-2433, press inquiries 301-496-4461
Fax: 301-402-2700
Web: www.nih.gov

The National Institutes of Health promote and conduct bio-medical research into the causes and prevention of diseases, and furnish information to health professionals and the public.

Other Associations/Organizations

American College of Sports Medicine
401 W. Michigan St.
Indianapolis, IN 46202-3233
Phone: 317-637-9200
Fax: 317-634-7817
Web: www.acsm.org
This 17,500-member organization integrates scientific research, education, and practical applications of sports medicine and exercise science to maintain and improve physical performance, fitness, health, and quality of life. The ACSM also certifies fitness and exercise specialists and instructors.

American Medical Association
515 N. State St.
Chicago, IL 60610
Phone: 312-464-5000
Fax: 312-464-4184
Web: www.ama-assn.org
The AMA is the largest medical organization in the country, consisting of 297,000 medical doctors. The AMA publishes *The Journal of the American Medical Association* and disseminates scientific information to members and the public.

American Psychiatric Association
1400 K Street, NW
Washington, D.C. 20005
Phone: 202-682-6000, press inquiries 202-682-6142
Fax: 202-682-6850
Web: http://www.psych.org

This 39,000-member organization consists solely of psychiatrists and provides press referrals for experts.

American Psychological Association
750 First Street, NE
Washington, D.C. 20002-4242
Phone: 202-336-5510 or 800-374-2721
Fax: 202-336-6069
Web: http://www.apa.org
This 151,000-member association promotes psychology as a science, profession, and means of helping humanity; good source for psychology experts.

American Psychotherapy Association
2750 E. Sunshine St.
Springfield, MO 65804
Phone: 417-823-0173 or 800-205-9165
Fax: 417-823-9959
Web: http://www.americanpsychotherapy.com
The organization promotes continuing education and training for psychotherapists.

American Public Health Association
800 I St., NW
Washington, D.C. 20001
Phone: 202-777-2742
Fax: 202-777-2534
Web: www.apha.org
This association consists of health care professionals, educators, environmentalists, social workers, industrial hygienists, and individuals; maintains information on all aspects of health care and education; and conducts research on the causes and origin of communicable diseases.

Association of Reproductive Health Professionals
2401 Pennsylvania Avenue, NW, Suite 350
Washington, D.C. 20037-1718
Phone: 202-466-3825
Fax: 202-466-3826
The ARHP consists of more than 2,000 professionals in the field of reproductive health; maintains a speakers bureau and sponsors clinical and public education programs.

Center for Patient Advocacy
1350 Beverly Rd., #108
McLean, VA 22101
Phone: 703-748-0400 or 800-846-7444
Fax: 703-748-0402
Web: www.patientadvocacy.org
The center represents patients and is committed to ensuring that they have access to up-to-the-minute health care.

The Information Exchange
120 N. Main St.
New City, NY 10956
Phone: 845-634-0050
Fax: 845-634-1690
The organization provides information for individuals with chronic mental/emotional disorders including mental illnesses, personality disorders, and emotional problems.

Institute for Health Care Research and Policy
2233 Wisconsin Ave., NW, #525
Washington, D.C. 20007
Phone: 202-687-0880
Fax: 202-687-3110
Web: www.georgetown.edu/research/ihcrp/
The institute is a research branch of Georgetown University and

includes interests in quality care, cost effectiveness, managed care, health privacy, and access to care.

Writers' Organizations and Other Resources

American Medical Writers Association
40 West Gude Dr., No. 101
Rockville, MD 20850-1192
Phone: 301-294-5303
Fax: 301-294-9006
Web: http://www.amwa.org
This 4,100-member organization includes medical writers, editors, public relations and pharmaceutical personnel, educators, publishers, and others concerned with communications in medicine and allied sciences. The AMWA publishes a directory of members available for freelance work.

National Association of Science Writers
P.O. Box 890
Hedgeville, WV 25427
Phone: 304-754-5077
Fax: 304-754-5076
Web: www.nasw.org
This 2,065-member organization includes writers and editors of science news for the public.

Health Writer's Handbook
by Barbara Gastel, M.D. (Iowa State University Press, 1998)
Excellent guide to writing about health; includes resources.

CHAPTER 6

Bananas to Blintzes

Writing About Diet, Nutrition & Food

The Basics: What You Need to Know

According to the U.S. Centers for Disease Control, a whopping 55 percent of adult Americans are now classified as over-weight—and that figure continues to grow, pardon the pun. Not surprisingly, every year a new crop of diet books arrives in book-stores. Quick weight-loss plans have long been popular in women's, men's, and fitness magazines, and will continue to be so. Yet Americans also love to read about—and enjoy—food, whether it's a gourmet meal for two, a simple family meal, or a backyard barbecue for the whole gang.

And there's more to writing about nutrition than simply describing the latest fad diet and whether it works. There is also a growing interest in articles about how nutrition can improve your health and reduce your risk of disease. And, specialized fields like sports nutrition and geriatric nutrition are gaining attention. Food writing—whether it's developing recipes aimed at middle-class families living on budgets or running down the latest cooking trend for higher-end gourmands—is another lucrative area for those who specialize in it. If you have experience in any of these areas—or if you just love food—this may be a specialty for you to consider.

Nuts and Bolts:
How to Write About Diet, Nutrition, and Food

Build Your Background

It takes more than the ability to whip together a delicious homemade dinner in less than ten minutes to be a successful food or nutrition writer. If you don't have any specialized background in this area, you may want to develop it before you begin pitching ideas.

"If you're writing about food, cook and learn about food," says freelancer Claire Walter of Boulder, Colorado, who writes about food, snow sports, and travel. "So if writing restaurant reviews is going to become your specialty, it's not a bad thing to spend a little time getting a job in a restaurant, to get a behind-the-scenes look at whatever your field is."

If you've worked in a restaurant, attended a culinary institute, or been a chef, you have a leg up on other freelancers. Even reading a few basic books on food and nutrition can help give you a handle on cooking techniques, what nutrients like vitamins and minerals are, and basic terminology.

Consider the Audience

When you're coming up with story ideas, think about the purpose of your story before you write the query or the article itself. Will it be a service-oriented piece explaining why readers

Build Relationships with Your Editors

Writing is like any other job—you need to build relationships with people.

A good editor should be cultivated like any other good client. I talk to my editors a lot. I don't waste their time, but I take any opportunity to talk to them in person, whether it's a visit or a phone call.

And I try to understand their job situations so I know when their deadlines are—and I make it clear that I know that. I show respect for their time and show respect for them.

I also send thank you notes and always follow up on a deadline to make sure it came through on e-mail—and to check if there's anything else I can do to make the story better or to help them.

—cont. on next page

should eat more omega-3 and omega-6 fats, offering ways to incorporate foods that contain them into their diets? An article comparing the quality of mail-order steaks? Or a round-up of recipes aimed at busy moms?

Also consider the audience you're writing for. If you're doing a piece on five new ways to prepare chicken for a magazine like *Family Circle*, you'll probably focus on ease of preparation, low ingredient cost, and taste that both adults and children will like. For a piece for *Gourmet*, however, you'll want to take a more upscale approach, both in terms of the ingredients themselves and in the cooking and preparation.

"You're not going to have really exotic recipes for a magazine like *Woman's Day*," agrees Diana Luger, a food writer based in Chicago. "Whereas with *Bon Appetit*, you have to assume you're dealing with a very sophisticated audience and that you're not going to have to explain certain basic terms to them. You can't talk down to them, either."

Think Seasonal

A lot of food-based writing is seasonally oriented. Obviously, most people don't want to spend hours in the kitchen making hearty soups and stews during the hottest months of the year. And during the winter months, some fruits and vegetables may be more difficult to come by. Coming up with a holiday or seasonal theme for your articles, whether it's Christmas, St. Patrick's Day, Halloween, or Lent—or for graduations, picnics, or tailgates—will also increase your chance of selling the idea.

"I would say a vast majority of food writing is seasonally oriented, and I think people miss out on those opportunities," says Luger. "You tend to think of Christmas in October and November, but editors are thinking about it in May or June, or earlier. Those articles are some of the hardest to write, but they're the ones editors are always looking for, because they've been doing it for 20 years." Look for a fresh viewpoint or a new angle on a tried-and-true topic to get your foot in the door.

Stay Trendy

Foods go in and out of fashion, just like clothing styles. Right now, millions of Americans are interested in lowering their fat intake. And many more are limiting the amount of carbohydrates they consume by switching to high-protein diets. Some are focusing on eating foods in their natural state, others are eliminating sugar from their diets, and still others are enjoying a return to the "comfort foods" they grew up with. Stay in touch with what's hot both in diets and food, and use that information to pitch timely story ideas.

"You need to find the trends coming up through the food service area before they hit the streets and before the average person knows about them," says Luger. "There are a lot of food service magazines that are geared to restaurant owners or people who package food, and I recommend people read those.

"Trendiness—in the sense of ingredients and sauces and styles of cooking—is cyclical. For example, you might want to do a recipe with chipotles. They're wonderful but they're not the hot trendy thing anymore." Luger also attends food shows and talks to local chefs to keep up on new ingredients and cooking styles.

Do Your Homework

When you're writing about nutrition, it's important to "know what you don't know," says Ed Blonz, a researcher and nutrition writer in Kensington, California. "I find that nutrition is something that everyone feels a sense of familiarity with because we all eat," says Blonz. "And also, there's a logic involved with 'this is good' and 'this is bad.' Without understanding the science behind it, people can get the mindset that they have more of a

Build Relationships

—cont. from previous page

I really take a lot of time to understand their end of the business, so I can match my performance to that.

For instance, one editor I work with has to pitch ideas for his section to his bigwig editor once a month . . . and he likes to have as many ideas as he can.

As soon as I found that out, I started sending him five ideas at a time, before that meeting, so he can take all of them in.

It saves him time and gives him something to show his boss which makes him look good—and it creates a built-in opportunity for me.

I usually sell all five ideas.
—Polly Campbell, Beaverton, Oregon

grasp than they really do. So not knowing the limits of your knowledge might lead you to accept basic intuitive explanations that have no scientific validity."

That's why most editors will insist that you back up any nutrition claims with copies of studies, research articles, and the like. If you don't have a background in nutrition, invest in a textbook that covers the basics; you might also take an entry-level nutrition course at your local college.

Find the Experts

When you're researching stories, be wary of any claims that sound too good to be true. "Be careful with the Internet," says Blonz. "It's fraught with commercial interests that are being masked as unbiased information."

So how do you separate fact from fiction, and helpful information from hype? By asking your sources to back up any claims they make. If you interview a researcher who says that his study proves that adding red pepper to food can help you lose weight, press for details about his work. What kind of study was involved? How much red pepper was used? How much weight did people lose? Were the study subjects even human? (You'd be amazed at the number of nutrition studies cited as conclusive by some "experts" that in fact involved rats or other animals.)

It helps to start developing a list of expert sources who know what's happening in the field. Associations like the American Dietetic Association will refer you to registered dietitians who have backgrounds in particular areas. You can also check with local colleges and universities to learn what types of research they're conducting. If you're working on a story and need an expert, call a major university or hospital and ask for their public affairs department; they can usually hook you up with a qualified person.

"Read as much as you can of other writers and scientists who are doing what you want to do," says Blonz. "You start getting an idea of who's who. Every time you see someone who is saying something that makes sense, write their name down, and you'll start to compile lists of people you can use as sources on the various aspects of nutrition and food."

Be Daring

Food writing isn't for everyone. If you're a vegetarian or even a picky eater, you might want to consider another specialty. To write about food, you have to keep an open mind about new tastes, cooking styles, and trends. "You have to be daring, and I think anyone who wants to write about food is," says Walter. "You can't turn your nose up at vast categories of cooking. But I suspect that anyone who doesn't have an adventuresome palate won't want to write about food anyway."

Be careful of your own biases, too. While I'm a vegetarian, I've written plenty of articles that talk about the nutritional benefits of eating beef, for example. I can't let my personal preferences overshadow the writing and reporting I do. While I might not believe all of the claims that some of the fad diet stories I've written promise, I can still report and write the story accurately, and leave it to readers to judge on their own.

Get Out of the House

If you do a lot of food or recipe writing, you may spend a lot of time in your own kitchen developing and testing recipes. But attending meetings or seminars can help you stay abreast of what's happening in the fields of nutrition and food, and may help you nail more work as well.

"Network, network, network," says Walter. "You never know where referrals will come from, and you never know who will call because you met at a conference, or because you were at a workshop together."

Be Clear

Articles about food and nutrition must also be accurate and easy to understand. Be as specific as you can. If you're writing about fiber, for example, don't just say "it's important to include more fiber in your diet." Instead, say "Most dietitians recommend that adults eat between 25 and 35 grams of fiber a day." Then give ways that readers can do that, or include examples of how much fiber common foods contain.

Obviously, when writing recipes, you must specify the exact amounts of ingredients. List them in the order they are used, and include any special cooking or preparation tools—nonstick pans, for example—as well as a list of the steps to take to put the recipe together. "You always want to list the first ingredient you use first, and do it in a very systematic way," says Luger. "You want to make things as concise and clear as possible. And consider your audience. If you're writing for *Woman's Day*, you might want to explain something more in depth than if writing a general cookbook."

Tales from the Front: Leslie Pepper

Leslie Pepper (yes, that's her real name) writes about diet and nutrition, fitness, and health from her home in Merrick, New York. Formerly an editor at *New Woman* magazine, she started freelancing in 1996, and she offers this advice for others who want to write about diet and nutrition:

- *Educate yourself.* Pepper was originally a fitness editor but started covering nutrition topics while still at *New Woman*. If you don't have a background in food or nutrition, taking a class in the basics will bring you up to speed and identify story ideas as well.

- *Check out your experts.* Just because someone wrote a book doesn't mean he or she is an authority on food or nutrition, warns Pepper. Instead of using book authors, she calls hospitals, universities, and associations like the American Dietetic Association to find nutrition sources for stories.

- *Consider the market.* A diet story for a magazine like *Family Circle* will have a different angle than one written for a trendier women's magazine like *Marie Claire*, for example. The former will be more focused on the basics, while the latter may be more interested in incorporating the latest research findings. Some magazines prefer to run the latest "fad" diets, too, while others prefer a more moderate, conservative approach to weight-loss regimes.

- *Stay informed.* An easy way to keep up on what's happening in the field of diet and nutrition is by subscribing to e-mail newsletters like the ones produced by Tufts University and the Center for Science in the Public Interest.

- *Include anecdotes.* Many magazines like to feature real-life examples in their nutrition stories. Did your neighbor recently lose 20 pounds by following the latest diet? Have you found a way to sneak soy into your kids' meals without their even noticing? Look for anecdotes that you can use in your queries and articles.

The Markets: Where to Sell Your Work

Write about diet, nutrition, and food, and you'll find a wide variety of markets for your work. Some of the biggest include:

- *Cooking/food magazines*—there are a variety of these magazines aimed at everyone from gourmands to vegetarians. All cover cooking techniques, food trends, nutrition research, and other related subjects.

- *General interest magazines*—encompass a broad range of topics including new breakthroughs in nutrition, research, food trends, cooking techniques, and other related areas.

- *Trade journals*—trade journals aimed at food professionals vary in their coverage, but may be markets for the latest developments in nutrition and food. Trade magazines aimed at other industries such as those involving fitness and health also feature nutrition and food articles.

- *Women's and men's magazines*—these magazines cover a broad range of food, nutrition, and diet subjects, mostly service-oriented.

- *Parenting magazines*—all cover children's nutrition and related topics; many feature simple recipes, topics like packing healthier lunches, cooking with kids, and the like.

- *Health and fitness magazines*—similar to general interest magazines in terms of coverage; broad scope of nearly every nutrition-related topic. These markets tend to be aimed at more specialized audiences, however—women in their 20s and 30s for example, or men and women 50 and up—so keep that in mind when pitching stories.

- *Travel magazines*—many travel magazines include articles on the foods and cultures of different places; writing about food and travel is a natural combination.

- *Web sites*—many Web sites, not just health-focused ones, cover a variety of health topics. As with other on-line publications, stories tend to be shorter than in print markets and include quizzes, links to other sites, and other interactive features.

- *National/major newspapers*—all have food, nutrition, and/or cooking sections.

- *Regional/city magazines and newspapers*—like their national counterparts, regional and city publications also cover food and nutrition subjects, often with a local angle.

Other Useful Stuff

When researching stories about food, nutrition, and diet, you'll need to find and interview credentialed, reliable experts and consult research studies. Some of the organizations and governmental agencies that can provide you with information and experts are listed below:

On-line Resources

InteliHealth
www.intelihealth.com
Offers free e-mail newsletters on nutrition and related topics; Web site also includes basic nutrition information.

Newswise
http://www.newswise.com
Newswise offers free e-mail newsletters, maintains press releases and an on-line directory of experts.

Profnet
www.profnet.com
Search the on-line database or submit a query to find experts in particular areas; you can also sign up for free e-mail releases about new research and story ideas.

PubMed
http://www.ncbi.nlm.nih.gov/PubMed/
PubMed provides on-line access to the National Library of Medicine.

Reuters Health
http://www.reutershealth.com/
Site that includes daily news releases about health, medicine, and nutrition.

Tufts University Health & Nutrition Letter
http://healthletter.tufts.edu/home2.htm
Well-respected newsletter covers nutrition and health.

Government Agencies

Agricultural Research Service (part of USDA)
1400 Independence Ave, SW, Suite 302A
Washington, D.C. 20250-0300
Phone: 202-720-3656
Fax: 202-720-5427
Web: www.ars.usda.gov
This is a nationwide network of research centers that study human nutrition, and livestock and crop production, protection, and processing.

Cooperative State Research, Education and Extension Service (Agriculture Department)
1400 Independence Ave., SW, #305A
Washington, D.C. 20250-2201
Phone: 202-720-4423
Fax: 202-720-8907
Web: www.reeusdda.gov
This agency oversees county agents and operation of state offices that provide information on nutrition, diet, food-purchase budgeting, food safety, home gardening, and other consumer concerns.

Food and Drug Administration (FDA)
Center for Food Safety and Applied Nutrition
5100 Paint Branch Parkway
College Park, MD 20740-3835
Phone: 1-888-723-3366 (CFSAN Food and Information Center)
Web: www.cfsan.fda.gov

The FDA's Center for Food Safety and Applied Nutrition monitors the safety and labeling of food and cosmetic products. The FDA itself is responsible for developing standards of composition and quality of foods (except meat and poultry); develops safety regulations for foods, cosmetics, and drugs; monitors pesticide residues in foods; conducts food safety and nutrition research; and develops methods for measuring food additives, nutrients, pesticides, and other contaminants. Its Web site is www.fda.gov.

National Agricultural Library
Food and Nutrition Information Center
10301 Baltimore Avenue, #105
Beltsville, MD 20705-2351
Phone: 301-504-5719
Fax: 301-504-6409
Web: www.nal.usda.gov/fnic
The center serves individuals and agencies seeking information or educational materials on food and human nutrition; maintains a database of food and nutrition software and multimedia programs; provides reference services; and develops resource lists of health and nutrition publications.

Other Associations/Organizations

American Dietetic Association (ADA)
216 W. Jackson Boulevard
Chicago, IL 60606-6995
Phone: 312-899-0040
Fax: 312-899-1979
Web: http://eatright.org
This 64,000-member organization is made up of registered dietitians, dietetic technicians, and other professionals. The ADA promotes nutrition, health, and well-being, and publishes the *Journal of the American Dietetic Association*; it also offers

nutritional and statistical information to journalists, and referrals to ADA spokespersons for expert sources.

American Society for Clinical Nutrition
9650 Rockville Pike, #L3300
Bethesda, MD 20814-3998
Phone: 301-530-7110
Fax: 301-571-1863
Web: www.faseb.org/ascn
This organization consists of clinical nutritionists and supports research on the role of human nutrition in health and disease.

American Society for Nutritional Sciences
9650 Rockville Pike, #4500
Bethesda, MD 20814-3998
Phone: 301-530-7050
Fax: 301-571-1892
Web: www.nutrition.org
This organization consists of research scientists, and conducts research in nutrition and related fields.

Center for Science in the Public Interest
1875 Connecticut Avenue NW, #300
Washington, D.C. 20009-5728
Phone: 202-332-9110
Fax: 202-265-4954
Web: www.cspinet.org
This organization conducts research on food and nutrition. Its interests include eating habits, food safety regulations, food additives, organically produced foods, alcoholic beverages, and links between diet and disease.

International Food Information Council
1100 Connecticut Avenue, NW, #430
Washington, D.C. 20036

Phone: 202-296-6540
Fax: 202-296-6547
Web: www.ific.org
This organization includes food and beverage companies and manufacturers of food ingredients. It provides the media, health professionals, and consumers with scientific information about food safety, health, and nutrition.

National Center for Nutrition and Dietetics
216 W. Jackson Boulevard
Chicago, IL 60606-6995
Phone: 800-366-1655
Web: http://www.eatright.org/ncnd.html
Founded by the American Dietetic Association, the NCND provides scientifically based food and nutrition information to the public.

National Restaurant Association
1200 17th St., NW
Washington, D.C. 20036
Phone: 202-331-5900
Fax: 202-331-2429
Web: www.restaurant.org
This trade organization consists of more than 52,000 member companies representing more than 254,000 restaurants. It maintains statistics on the trade.

Nutrition Education Association
P.O. Box 20301
3647 Glen Haven
Houston, TX 77225
Phone: 713-665-2946
This organization educates the public about the importance of good nutrition as a means of acquiring and maintaining good health.

Physicians Committee for Responsible Medicine
5100 Wisconsin Avenue, NW, #400
Washington, D.C. 20016
Web: www.pcrm.org
This organization is made up of health care professionals, medical students, and laypersons interested in preventive medicine. It conducts clinical research, educational programs, and public information campaigns.

Society for Nutrition Education
1001 Connecticut Ave, NW, Suite 528
Washington, D.C. 20036
Phone: 202-452-8534 or 800-235-6690
Fax: 202-452-8536
Web: http://www.sne.org
This 1800-member organization includes nutrition educators from the fields of dietetics, public health, home economics, medicine, industry, and education.

Writers' Organizations and Other Resources

Association of Food Journalists
38309 Genesee Lake Road
Oconomowoc, WI 53066
Phone: 262-965-3251
Web: www.afjonline.com
This 300-member organization includes both freelance food journalists and those on staff at newspapers, magazines, and Internet services.

International Association of Culinary Professionals
304 W. Liberty St., Suite 201
Louisville, KY 40202
Phone 502-581-9786 or 800-928-4227
Fax: 502-589-3602

Web: www.iacp.org
This organization includes food writers, cookbook authors, cooking school owners, chefs, caterers, teachers, food stylists, and photographers; one section is devoted to food writers and editors.

International Food, Wine and Travel Writers Association (IFWTWA)
P.O. Box 8249
Calabasas, CA 91372
Phone: 818-999-9959
Fax: 818-347-7545
Web: http://www.ifwtwa.org
Founded in 1956, this 435-member organization consists of professional food, wine, and travel journalists in 28 countries; travel and hospitality industry organizations are associate members.

The Resource Guide for Food Writers
by Gary Allen (Routledge, 1999)
This 304-page book is loaded with information on organizations, periodicals, Web sites, databases, and other sources for food and nutrition writers.

CHAPTER 7

Show Me the Money

Writing About Business & Finance

The Basics: What You Need to Know

Write well about business, and you'll find no shortage of markets for your work. General interest magazines, inflight magazines, finance-oriented publications, newspapers, and Web sites are some of the many outlets for stories about business, trade, and commerce. In addition, thousands of trade journals are actively looking for freelance writers who can report on their industries and translate the latest developments in local, national, and international business to readers.

The consumer finance area is another growing field for freelancers. Here, stories run the gamut from how newlyweds can communicate about money to how to save for your children's college education to smart investment strategies for the future. While it doesn't hurt to have a good background in business or finance, any writer with experience in a specific industry or profession can use that knowledge to crack these rewarding markets and create his or her own niche.

Nuts and Bolts:
How to Write About Business and Finance

Don't Be Afraid

First things first. Want to write about business, but worry you don't know enough about it? While there is a learning curve involved, it's not as complicated as you may think. "I think a lot of reporters are scared of business writing—I find I get a lot of work because there aren't as many people out there who feel comfortable writing about business," says freelancer Margaret Littman of Chicago, who writes about business and health subjects.

"Yes, business writing is technical and you have to know what you're talking about—you have know what an earnings statement is, for example, and know what the terminology is—but people think of it as a specialized niche, and it's not. Everyone runs a business or works for a business. And every business issue affects almost everyone."

Use Your Experience

Many writers use their backgrounds in business and industry to get started in this field. Joshua Karp, a writer based in Evanston, Illinois, was finishing his master's degree in journalism when he nabbed his first business story. He had worked in advertising and marketing as well as for a manufacturing and distribution company before returning to school; he used that fact to help convince an editor at *Crain's Chicago Business* to give him an assignment. The first assignment turned into others, and by the time he graduated, he was doing two stories a month for the publication.

Karp's next regular gig was for a dot-com company, where he wrote a 700-word piece on high-tech business once a week. "I got to pick my beat, and I chose to cover high-tech business. I worked for them for six months, basically covering the intersection between creativity and technology," says Karp. "That was a great experience. It was great to get the money and to have the work, but I also got to grow a lot as a business writer."

He covered topics such as video production, Web design, and advertising, and in just a few months' time had developed expertise in business and technology. Two years later, he specializes in business-related subjects and makes a good living as a freelancer.

Know Your Stuff

When you're writing about business, you have to be a thorough researcher. It's not enough to talk to only one person about a particular topic. Remember that your readers are going to have a vested interest in the subject and often already know a lot about the topics you're writing about.

If you're missing critical information or don't understand a concept, don't try to write around it. You have to understand it, or your ignorance will be reflected in your stories—and people will notice. "You don't want to get caught with your pants down," warns Karp. "I find with business there are a lot of angles, and you've got to make sure that you're getting the core of what people are saying . . . if you don't get it, it really shows."

If business is a new topic for you, get some basic guidebooks and reference books to educate yourself about some of the terms that you'll be using. Personal finance books like *Making the Most of Your Money* by Jane Bryant Quinn (Simon & Schuster, 1997) can also be helpful references and trigger story ideas as well.

Don't Be Afraid to Be Creative

Think business stories have to be as exciting as watching paint dry? Think again—and strive to enhance your stories with creativity whenever possible.

"Business stories don't need to be dry, boring stuff," agrees Kristin Baird Rattini, a freelancer who writes for trade and custom publications. Rattini does a lot of profiles of small-business owners, and admits that it can be challenging to come up with a new approach to each one. Still, she always looks for something that makes the story unique. Consider a story she was assigned on a new paint line; she had to interview a True Value retailer in southwest Utah who was selling the paint.

"It could have been a very dry story—'This is the paint,' 'This is how they're selling it,' et cetera," says Rattini.

"But because of the retailer's location in the Wild, Wild West and because of a confrontational encounter he had with another paint retailer in town, I was able to spin it with a Wild West theme and really add creativity and flair to it.

"It's up to you to find the creative potential in each story. Know that you don't have to do a rote, boring, dry business story just because it seems like a boring topic initially."

Karp says he always tries to have a story line running through his articles. "I want it to have as much of a narrative flow as humanly possible," he says. "At the very least, it should have a lead and an ending, and some kind of narrative flow that runs from one end to the other with a lot of reporting in the middle."

He also likes to surprise his readers. For example, in one of his articles on home offices, he used a lead that described a huge corporate office fully equipped with the latest in cutting-edge technology. In closing the lead, he noted that there were also toys and Cheerios strewn about on the floor—the business owner's office is located in her daughter's nursery.

Negotiate More Money

Basically if I feel like I can get more or I deserve more, I ask for more.

If someone says, "We can pay you $1,000 for this project," and I think that's a little low, I'll say, "Can you go a little bit higher?"

I'll explain my request. I'll point out the project is going to require a lot of interviews or a lot of research. I give them some reason why I feel I should be paid more. That's important.

I won't name a figure but I'll say, "If you can pay a little bit more, I'd appreciate it."

I've done this a number of times . . . and magazines have agreed to pay me more right on the spot.

—cont. on next page

One of the best ways to come up with story ideas is to track what local companies are doing and watch for business trends. Talk to your chamber of commerce, read the business section of the local papers, and keep your ears open for possible subjects. For stories on personal finance topics, remember: Evergreen subjects—such as saving for retirement and investment dos and don'ts—never go out of style. Look at the financial issues your own family is facing or the topics you talk about with your friends.

"There's an endless well of stories out there being run on credit cards, credit card debt, and saving for college. They're perennial stories because families grow into the stories every year. So there's always a market for those topics," says Rattini.

"Consumer finance is something that is both familiar and foreign. It's familiar because we may be going through it on our own, but we may not understand what we're going through. Look at what you're experiencing personally to find some ideas, and at the very least, some lessons to work from."

Be Extra Accurate

When you're writing about business, you can't fudge numbers or guess when you should have specific data. If your stories include mistakes, you'll have a short-lived career as a business writer. On the other hand, if you develop a reputation for accuracy, you'll have no shortage of work.

Even simple mistakes can trip you up—miscalculating a percentage, for example. Even if it's basic math, double-check your work. And let your editor know how you came up with any figures (the editor will want to know the sources of data you cite anyway).

And if experts quote figures or statistics, ask them where the numbers came from and how they were calculated.

Know the Style Book

Does the publication you're writing for use Chicago or AP style? How does it identify people? Does it include ages or hometowns? Know the house style of the publications you write for, and you'll endear yourself to editors. "Knowing their house style on things is huge," agrees Karp. "At *Crain's*, the first reference is always 'Mr. or Ms. full name as appears on business card, full title, official name of company, and location.' It might be something like 'Hoffman Estates, Illinois-based Sears, Roebuck, and Company, Ltd.' They are really huge sticklers for that kind of stuff."

Don't Be Afraid to Ask—and Ask Again

If you're new to writing about business—or even if you're not—there may be times when sources use terms or language that you don't understand. Or maybe they're just not making any sense. Pin them down if necessary or ask them to clarify what they're saying.

"When you're interviewing business people, do not be afraid to ask them to explain," says Karp. "If you have to ask them five times to explain something, it's not because you're stupid—it's because they're not explaining it very well. Early on, that was a very intimidating aspect for me—talking to someone from a very large company and feeling like I was an idiot because I didn't understand what he was referring to. But oftentimes, they just assume that you know things about their sector of business that you don't."

"I think a lot of people are intimated to call a CEO, because their names are names you hear all the time and they are worth billions of dollars," agrees Littman. "It's important to not be intimated, just like you wouldn't be with any other source. It's sort of a hard thing at first, but once you do it for a while, you meet these guys and you figure out that they're normal."

Negotiate . . .

—cont. from previous page

And I've never lost an assignment for asking for more money.

In the business world, people negotiate fees for everything, and writers should be assertive about asking for more money if they feel they deserve it.

The worst that an editor can say is no. Then you still can decide if you want to work on that project anyway.

—Sam Greengard, Burbank, California

Use Anecdotes

It's much easier to bring a human perspective to business stories when you can cite examples of people and companies in your articles. "Look for the telling anecdotes," says Rattini. "Business stories very often get weighed down by expert opinions—'This is what an expert thinks business owners should do,' and 'This is how they should do that.' But the anecdotes can speak volumes, because they offer specific examples of how one person has put those theories into practice either successfully or not successfully."

Don't be afraid to ask your business sources to back up any claims they make as well. For example, Rattini often profiles independent grocery store owners for *IGA Grocergram*, a trade publication. "Just about every single store owner says that he prides himself on customer service. That's great lip service, but I press for specific examples. And those examples usually reveal how they've been able to put that into practice," she says.

"Maybe a meat department manager has been packaging meats in smaller packages for his senior citizens. Or a bakery manager offers free samples every day. Anecdotes give specific examples of how they've been able to put this into practice and brings a human element into an otherwise disembodied voice of an expert."

For another story on college students and credit card debt, Rattini found a college student who was graduating with a $16,000 credit-card balance to his name. "Jason, the student, mentioned that people should think about using debit cards because that helps control their spending," says Rattini.

"He gave me an example of something that several other experts had told me. But the fact that he himself had put it into practice made it a stronger recommendation. When you have someone who can tell about their own experiences, it gives an extra credibility to it instead of having an expert saying it."

Consider Your Audience

Remember to keep your readers in mind as you write. If you're writing for a trade or business-specific publication, your readers probably have more background in business subjects than if you're writing for a consumer publication aimed at a more general audience.

"You assume a different level of knowledge for a consumer publication. With trades, you're pretty much assuming that you're writing for people who work in the industry, and they have at least a basic knowledge of operations, standard practices, and terminology," says Rattini. "Be prepared to give a more thorough explanation and perhaps use simpler language and more examples in a consumer magazine than in a trade magazine."

While the editor may dictate the format of the piece, don't be afraid to use a FAQ (Frequently Asked Questions) or a Q&A format if possible. Both help break complex subjects into simpler, easy-to-understand chunks, says Rattini.

Tales from the Front: Ari Tye Radetsky

Ari Tye Radetsky of Denver, Colorado, has been freelancing for five years. He used his background in computer consulting to establish himself as a freelancer, writing about technological subjects. While he covers a variety of subjects, business and technology are his primary specialties. He offers this advice for freelancers new to writing about business:

- *Be accurate in your reporting.* Remember that your readers will often know as much—or more than—you do about their particular industry or business, and they'll notice if you make mistakes.

- *Root out the PR talk and jargon.* Don't fall into the trap of using terms that may have some meaning in a particular industry but don't have a meaning to the average reader—or don't mean what they say. If a business executive says, "This has a fantastic ROI (return on investment)," nail him down and ask how he's measuring that ROI.

- *Be careful with your terminology.* For example, "markets" and "economies" mean similar things but they are not synonyms.

- *Double-check any information you get off the Internet.* You can follow up with the marketing or PR department of a company to confirm any information on their site—it takes little time and your editors will appreciate it when it comes to fact-checking.

- *Develop multiple story ideas to maximize your research time.* For example, you might write about copy-protected CDs from the business side of it, from the technology side, and from the recording-industry side. It usually takes little time to spin more than one story out of the same basic research.

The Markets: Where to Sell Business Writing

Business writers have a broad range of markets to choose from, and rates vary depending on the size of the market. While trade magazines tend to pay less than consumer publications, they often provide a steady source of work for freelancers. Some of the biggest markets for business-related writing include:

- *General interest magazines*—broad range of coverage including business strategies, the economy, personal finance and investing, business profiles, and other related areas.

- *Business and personal finance magazines*—these magazines cover all aspects of business, industry, commerce, and/or personal finance.

- *Professional and trade journals*—depending on the journal, may have a narrower range of interest; many trade magazines cover specific industries or businesses.

- *Women's and men's magazines*—these magazines cover a broad range of subjects including personal finance and topics like saving for college and retirement, investing, buying a home or car, and the like.

- *Inflight magazines*—these publications are published by airlines for travelers to read and usually focus on business subjects.

- *Business-oriented Web sites*—these markets cover a variety of business topics. As with other on-line publications, stories tend to run shorter than in print markets and include quizzes, links to other sites, and other interactive features.

- *National/major newspapers*—cover all aspects of business and industry.

- *Regional/city magazines and newspapers*—like their national counterparts, regional and city publications also cover a broad range of business-related topics, often with a local angle.

Other Useful Stuff

If you choose to specialize in business writing, you may want to start by focusing on a particular trade, industry, or niche. Developing a Rolodex of experts, analysts, and other professionals will help you research and report stories accurately. Some possible story sources are listed below:

On-line Resources

Bloomberg.com
www.bloomberg.com
Breaking news from Bloomberg, an information-services, news, and media company.

Business Week On-line
www.businessweek.com
On-line version of the publication.

Hoover's On-line
www.hoovers.com
Business and financial news from Hoover's, a business consulting company.

Nasdaq Stock Market
www.nasdaq.com
Detailed market information from Nasdaq.

Newsdesk
www.newsdesk.com
Newsdesk offers free e-mail newsletters on business and other topics.

Newswise
http://www.newswise.com
Newswise offers free e-mail newsletters on business; maintains press releases and an online directory of experts.

New York Stock Exchange online
www.nyse.com
News, current data, and other information.

The New York Times On-line
www.nytimes.com
On-line version of the publication.

Profnet
www.profnet.com
Search the on-line database or submit a query to find experts in

particular areas; you can also sign up for free e-mail releases about new research and story ideas.

Reuters
www.reuters.com
Business information and breaking news.

Wall Street Journal On-line
www.wsj.com
On-line version of the publication.

Governmental Agencies, Associations, and Organizations

Commerce Department
14th Street and Constitution Ave. NW, #5854
Washington, D.C. 20230
Phone: 202-482-2112
Press: 202-482-2741
Fax: 202-482-4883
Web: www.doc.gov
The Commerce Department acts as a principal adviser to the U.S. president on federal policy affecting industry and commerce. It promotes economic growth, trade, and technological development, and provides economic statistics, research, and analysis. Staff also answer questions about commerce and business.

Small Business Administration
409 3rd St. SW, #7000
Washington, D.C. 20416
Phone: 202-205-6605 or 800-827-5722
Press: 202-205-6740
Fax: 202-205-6802

Web: www.sba.gov
The SBA is the U.S. government's principal advocate of small business interests through financial, investment, procurement, and management assistance, and counseling.

Treasury Department
1500 Pennsylvania Ave. NW, #3330
Washington, D.C. 20220
Phone: 202-622-1100
Information 202-622-1260
Fax: 202-622-0073
Web: www.ustreas.gov
The Treasury Department formulates and recommends domestic and international financial, economic, tax, and broad fiscal policies.

Other Associations/Organizations

American Advertising Federation
1101 Vermont Avenue NW, Suite 500
Washington, D.C. 20005-6306
Phone: 202-898-0089
Fax: 202-898-0159
Web: http://www.aaf.org
The American Advertising Foundation consists of 45,000 members and works to advance the business of advertising; operates a speakers' bureau.

American Bankers Association
1120 Connecticut Ave. NW
Washington, D.C. 20036
Phone: 202-663-5000 or 800-BANKERS
Fax: 202-663-7543
Web: www.aba.com
This 8,000-member organization includes primarily commercial

banks and trust companies; the combined assets of members represent about 90 percent of the U.S. banking industry.

American Finance Association
University of California Berkeley
Hass School of Business
545 Student Services Building
Berkeley, CA 94720-1900
Phone: 510-642-2397
Fax: 510-642-2397
Web: www.afajof.org
The AFA has 7,500 members and consists of college and university professors of economics and finance, bankers, treasurers, analysts, financiers, and others interested in financial problems; publishes the *Journal of Finance*.

American Institute of Certified Public Accountants
1211 Avenue of the Americas
New York, NY 10036-8775
Phone: 212-596-6200 or 888-777-7077
Fax: 212-596-6213
Web: www.aicpa.org
This is the professional society of accountants who are certified by U.S. states and territories; includes more than 316,000 members.

American Management Association
1601 Broadway
New York, NY 10019-7420
Phone: 212-586-8100
Fax: 212-903-8168
Web: www.ama.org
This 80,000-member organization provides worldwide educational forums where members learn practical business skills; offers continuing education through their publishing program.

America's Community Bankers
900 19th St. NW, Suite 400
Washington, D.C. 20006
Phone: 202-857-3100
Fax: 202-296-8716
Web: www.acbankers.org
This 2,100-member organization consists of savings and loan associations, savings banks, cooperative banks, and state and local savings and loan associations in U.S. states and territories.

Associated Credit Bureaus
1090 Vermont Avenue NW, Suite 200
Washington, D.C. 20005-4905
Phone: 202-371-0910
Fax: 202-371-1034
Web: www.acb-credit.com
The ACB is an international association of credit-reporting and collection-service offices.

Chamber of Commerce of the United States
1615 H St. NW
Washington, D.C. 20062
Phone: 202-659-6000
Fax: 202-463-5836
Web: www.uschamber.com
The chamber is a national federation of 219,200 business organizations and companies; it maintains a speakers' bureau, compiles statistics, and conducts research programs.

Council of Better Business Bureaus
4200 Wilson Boulevard, Suite 800
Arlington, VA 22203-1838
Phone: 703-276-0100
Fax: 703-525-8277
Web: www.bbb.org, www.bbbonline.org, www.doanddontz.org

The council is supported by 325 companies and 132 local Better Business Bureaus; it monitors truth and accuracy of national advertising claims, develops information on national charitable organizations, provides information to consumers, publishes consumer education leaflets, and settles consumer complaints through arbitration and other means.

Credit Union National Association
P.O. Box 431
Madison, WI 53701
Phone: 608-231-4000 or 800-356-9655
Fax: 608-231-4263
Web: www.cuna.org/data/
This 10,000-member organization serves more than 90 percent of credit unions in the United States through state leagues; total membership of more than 77 million people.

Financial Planning Association
5775 Glenridge Dr. NE, Suite B-300
Atlanta, GA 30328-5364
Phone: 404-845-0011 or 800-322-4237
Fax: 404-845-3660
Web: www.fpanet.org
This organization has 17,000 members in 22 countries and is made up of individuals involved in financial planning. The FPA maintains a speakers' data bank and compiles statistics.

Franchise Consultants International Association
5147 S. Angela Rd.
Memphis, TN 38117
Phone: 901-368-3361 or 901-368-3333
Fax: 901-368-1144
The association includes individuals and corporations involved in franchising, including attorneys, consultants, brokers, sales personnel, suppliers, universities, advertisers, and developers;

serves as clearinghouse for approved literature on franchising and compiles statistics.

National Association of Manufacturers
1331 Pennsylvania Ave. NW, Suite 600
Washington, D.C. 20004
Phone: 202-637-3000 or 800-814-8468
Fax: 202-637-3182
Web: www.nam.org
The NAM represents the manufacturing industries' views on national and international problems to government; affiliated with 150 local and state trade associations of manufacturers through the National Industrial Council.

National Association of Securities Dealers
1735 K St. NW
Washington, D.C. 20006-1506
Phone: 202-728-8000
Fax: 202-293-6260
Web: www.nasdr.com/1000.asp
This 5,500-member association consists of firms doing business with the public.

National Retail Federation
325 7th St. NW, Suite 1100
Washington, D.C. 20004
Phone: 202-783-7971 or 800-NRF-HOW2
Fax: 202-737-2849
Web: www.nrf.com
The National Retail Federation represents 50 state retail associations, several dozen national retail associations, and large and small corporate members of the retail industry; it also conducts retailing-related conferences.

Securities Industry Association
120 Broadway, 35th Floor
New York, NY 10271-0080
Phone: 212-608-1500
Fax: 212-608-1604
Web: www.sia.com
This 760-member organization includes investment bankers, securities underwriters, and stocks and bonds dealers. It compiles statistics on investments, securities markets, and related matters.

Writers' Organizations and Other Resources

American Society of Business Publication Editors
710 East Ogden Avenue, Suite 600
Naperville, IL 60563-8603
Phone: 630-579-3288
Fax: 630-369-2488
Web: www.asbpe.org
This 400-member organization includes executive, managing, and working editors of business, trade, and technical publications.

Society of American Business Editors and Writers
c/o University of Missouri, School of Journalism
76 Gannett Hall
Columbia, MO 65211
Phone: 573-882-7862 or 573-882-8985
Fax: 573-884-1372
Web: www.sabew.org
This 3,200-member organization consists of active business, economic, and financial newswriters and editors for magazines, newspapers, and other publications; also includes business and journalism professors. Maintains a résumé bank and publishes *The Business Journalist*.

CHAPTER 8

Calling All Web-Heads

Writing About Technology

The Basics: What You Need to Know

New developments in technology have changed the way we work, the way we play, and the way we live—and have produced a huge demand for freelancers who can report and write on technology-based subjects. As technology's influence continues, so will the need for savvy tech writers. Even the dot-com crashes at the onset of the millennium haven't eliminated the market—technology is still making a major impact on our daily lives and will continue to be a hot beat for writers who can cover it.

While it is a specialized field that requires some working knowledge of technical issues, you needn't be a network administrator to pitch and write articles aimed at business owners or consumers. The key to turning your interest in technology into high-paying assignments is having an understanding of how technology works and being able to communicate sometimes complicated concepts in simple language.

Nuts and Bolts:
How to Write About Technology

You Needn't Be a Geek

While having some background in technology doesn't hurt, you needn't be a techie whiz to create a specialty in this area. Ask Monique Cuvelier, a freelancer in Boston, who has been writing about technology for more than seven years. "I think I was just one of the early people who didn't think technology was dorky, and I wasn't afraid to write about it, so I got some interesting stories placed," says Cuvelier. "It seemed like a logical outgrowth from the business writing I'd been doing. Maybe that's the key—for people not to have the idea that you have to wear tape on your glasses or know how to program COBOL before you write something about technology."

Still, though, it helps to have some knowledge of what you're writing about. "For example, I have no idea how to build a data warehousing system, but I know what it's supposed to do when it's built," says Cuvelier. The ability to learn about technology is also important, as is the ability to understand how the concepts you're writing about relate to the real world.

"You do have to have some foundation and some understanding of technology to write about it," says Sam Greengard, a freelancer who writes about technology and business in Burbank, California. "But you don't have to be a technical expert. I'm a tech generalist, so I try to have a broad knowledge base, and then use the analysts and experts and people like that to drill down."

Consider the Impact

Think of technology as a tool. Many people don't care about technology itself, but they do care about its impact on their lives and businesses. When writing about technology you need to think beyond how something functions and explain to readers how this will affect their lives. "Don't try to explain how everything works unless it's a technical pub where you need to do that," says Greengard. "It's better to humanize the story. Don't write about the technology—write about how it helps somebody or how it makes their life better.

"For example, you can't expect to write an article about personal digital assistants (PDAs), and explain how they work," says Greengard. "But what you can write about is what are their benefits, what are their problems, and should someone out there buy one—and if they already have one, how can they use it more effectively."

One of the most effective ways to enliven a technological story is by using some real-people or real-company examples. "Try to include case studies and anecdotes, as in any other kind of writing," says Greengard. "I think sometimes those case studies can tell more in a paragraph than a thousand words of explaining—because it's someone really doing it."

Avoid Jargon

Just because you're writing about technology doesn't mean your stories should be dry, technical, and laced with jargon. "Editors usually want a conversational tone and something that is easily understood and easily read," says Greengard. "That means boiling it down to simpler terms. You have to avoid acronyms and jargon and passive voice. When a story gets bogged down in jargon and acronyms and this, that, and the other thing, it becomes too vague and dense."

The catch is that you don't want to treat the readers like

they're morons, either. "There's a fine line when writing about technology. On one hand, often the readers know a lot more than you do, and you have to know what kind of obvious information not to include," says Cuvelier.

"But on the other hand, you have to know how to explain complicated systems in plain English—which is harder than it sounds. Too many tech articles sound like they're written for five-year-olds. You have to tell readers how something works without talking down to them."

Go to the Source(s)

When you're writing about technology, you'll want to develop your own Rolodex of experts to call upon. Possible sources include analysts, professors, engineers, software developers, and Webmasters. But while they may have access to information that you don't, remember that sources are likely to have their own agendas as well. If a software developer praises its latest product, ask for references of "real people" who are already using it. (Just keep in mind that a vendor is usually going to provide you with the names of people who will speak glowingly about their products, so you may have to look for independent sources as well.) In short, do rely on experts for up-to-date information, but don't take what they—or the people they send you to—say at face value.

Sometimes the most difficult part of a technology story is finding real-life examples to include. Local chambers of commerce and PR companies can often provide leads for possible sources, which can save writers time when they're facing a tight deadline. "I have a stable of PR contacts whom I can trust," says Lain Ehmann, a freelancer in Los Gatos, California. "If I'm looking for someone who, say, can talk about systems integration, and the PR agency has in the past referred a legitimate company that didn't make me look bad, I'll check back with them to find sources."

Nail Them Down

Even if you have a background in technology, expect to ask questions—and more questions—of the experts you interview. If you don't understand what an engineer or software developer is telling you, you won't be able to effectively explain it to readers later. "Don't let the technical people like engineers get away with some off-the-cuff answer that you don't understand," says Ehmann. "They're usually very accommodating if you say, 'Can you explain that again?' or 'What do you mean by that?'"

Accept that you probably won't understand every concept the first time it's explained to you, and don't worry about looking stupid. "Never be afraid to ask the 'stupid' questions," says Ehmann. "I think the temptation is to avoid asking the questions because you don't want to sound like an idiot. But the only way you sound like an idiot if you *don't* ask the questions and you write about it and get something wrong—and then your audience knows that you blew it."

Follow the Trends

In technology, trends come and go very quickly. It can be tough to stay current because the field changes so quickly. If you develop a niche within technology—whether it's covering distance learning, e-commerce, or wireless communication, for example—it helps you keep up-to-date without being overwhelmed.

Ehmann says she sets herself apart from other technology writers by continuing to seek out new markets and refine her focus as trends come and go. "Within the field of technology, there are many subspecialties, just as there are in any other field," says Ehmann. "While I can write about technology in general, mostly I write about the business of technology—meaning marketing, management, et cetera—rather than the technology itself."

Get Your Foot in the Door

If you know something about technology but haven't written about it before, the shorter front sections of magazines (called FOB, or "front of book") are good places for new writers to break in. Many technology magazines maintain editorial calendars, so request a copy of the calendar before you pitch ideas. You might suggest a column idea for a regular department, or a profile of a business or individual who is using technology in an unusual or different way.

"What editors want is someone who understands technology in general and can talk to the technical people and interview company representatives, and then write about the technology for their audience," says Ehmann.

Even if your technology expertise is limited to one area, you can use that as a selling point in your query. "Technology crosses so many different areas, from networking to e-commerce to software to hardware to telecommunications," says Ehmann. "Once you have a grounding in the basics, you can cross back and forth amongst those very easily."

Consider the Audience

As with any type of writing, you must keep the audience you're writing for in mind. There are four basic types of technological markets—consumer, trade, corporate, and custom publishing—and each is slightly different, says Greengard.

With consumer markets, the stories tend to be less technical. "For example, if people are sitting on an airplane or they're in their doctor's office reading a magazine article about personal digital assistants, they need to know why it's important to them," says Greengard. "So, I need to connect with the average Joe on the street."

With a business trade magazine, however, the audience is employers, employees, or both. "People in the business world

Think Per Hour, not Per Word

It's how much you make per hour—that's the key thing.

First, you have to understand what you want to make per year, and then do the math backwards to understand what you need to make per hour.

And after a while, you have a pretty good idea of how long a given project is going to take.

So there are times when I'll work for 50 cents a word or 30 cents a word—because I still can make $500 or $1,000 for an hour's worth of work.

There are other times when I won't touch a project that pays $3 a word—because I know I'm going to spend weeks or months being put through the meat grinder.

—Sam Greengard, Burbank, California

have very different needs, and they want more information—although again, not necessarily highly technical information," says Greengard. "But they need more information about how-to, like how to effectively use computers and technology. Again, the bottom line is how does it relate to them, how can it make their work better or easier."

Custom publications are a hybrid of sorts. Because they're sponsored by a particular company or organization, you may have to keep the publication's purpose in mind, as well as the audience you're writing for and how sophisticated it is.

Finally, with corporate publications, which are usually narrower both in scope and audience, the company's agenda controls the topics they cover, story angles, and the amount of technical detail included.

Stay Current

To write effectively about technology, you have to keep up with what's happening in the industry. Trade publications like *Information Week*, *Internet Week*, and *Internet World* can help keep you up to date. Consumer publications like *Business 2.0*, *Fast Company*, *Red Herring*, *Popular Science*, *Wired*, and *Upside* can also be helpful. When you're familiar not only with what's happening now but also with the possible implications, you're more likely to nail assignments.

"Technology is a very broad but also a very small world, and you see a lot of the same names crop up—it's very incestuous in terms of people going from one company to another," says Ehmann. "If you bring to an editor a history and an understanding of the broader landscape, you're that much more valuable. If you can write about not only wireless advertising but also why wireless advertising is better than Internet advertising—if you place it in context—it's very valuable. You have to keep on the current edge, just like the companies themselves, because there's always the next big thing. As a tech writer, you have to keep current so you can write about the next big thing."

Tales from the Front: W. Eric Martin

W. Eric Martin is a Boston-based freelancer who writes about a variety of subjects. While he doesn't consider himself a specialist per se, at least half of his articles concern some aspect of technology. He offers this advice to journalists who want to cover technology:

- *Make sure you're describing the technology accurately.* Ask questions about everything, even if you think you know what's going on. If you have any doubts or questions, ask the person interviewed or someone familiar with the technology to review what you've written—they can find mistakes more quickly than you can.

- *Get hands-on experience.* If you can actually use the technology, it helps you describe it more accurately. For example, Martin visited a plant in Rhode Island where laptop computers are recycled, which helped him write a more detailed story about the facility. He also was able to get access to the wireless network security system created for the 2002 Olympics, which gave him a different perspective when it came to writing the piece.

- *Define any jargon or terms the reader may not know.* If it's just a word or two, you can address it in the story; otherwise, you may want to include sidebars to explain concepts or how something works. If you're talking about a new technology, describe it in terms of something the readers will be familiar with.

- *Don't be taken in by hype.* There's way too much talk about "revolutionizing" industries and potential long-term results because of new technology. If you don't know what the effects of a new technology are going to be, don't oversell what you're talking about. Let the experts and people in the field speak for themselves. And instead of having a product's manufacturer or developer predict its usefulness, ask people who actually use it.

The Markets: Where to Sell Technology Writing

You may be surprised at the range of markets for technology articles. Rates vary depending on the size of the market. Because of technology's continuing impact on business and industry, trade magazines are also a lucrative market for technology writers. Some of the biggest markets for technology-related writing and their areas of interest include:

- *General interest magazines*—broad range of coverage, including technology's impact on business and the economy, devices and technologies that make everyday life easier, the latest developments, and other related areas.

- *Technology magazines*—these magazines are devoted specifically to technology but have different focuses and audiences; read closely before pitching ideas.

- *Business magazines*—these magazines cover all aspects of technology as it relates to business and industry, including how-to, the pros and cons of different technologies, profiles, and the like.

- *Professional and trade journals*—depending on the journal, this may be a narrower range of interest; many trade magazines cover specific industries or businesses.

- *Women's and men's magazines*—these magazines cover technology as it relates to daily life, personal finance, recreation, parenting, and other subjects.

- *Business-oriented Web sites*—these markets cover a variety of technology topics, again focusing on how they affect business and industry. As with other on-line publications, stories tend to run shorter than in print markets and include quizzes, links to other sites, and other interactive features.

- *National/major newspapers*—cover all aspects of technology and its implications for businesses and individuals.

- *Regional/city magazines and newspapers*—like their national counterparts, regional and city publications also cover a broad range of technology-related subjects, often with a local angle.

Other Useful Stuff

Because technology changes so quickly, many writers rely on Web sites, e-mail newsletters, and on-line sources to keep tabs on what's happening. Technology writers often must interview consultants, analysts, and other experts, and have found some of the following sources helpful.

Web Resources

Bloomberg.com
www.bloomberg.com
Breaking news from Bloomberg, an information-services, news, and media company.

Business Week On-line
www.businessweek.com
On-line version of the publication.

CNET.com
www.CNET.com
Site that includes information technology (IT) information and news; includes free newsletters.

Free Tech Mail
www.freetechmail.org
The site lists hundreds of free IT newsletters available on line.

Hoover's On-line
www.hoovers.com
Business and financial news from Hoover's, a business consulting company.

IDG.net
www.IDG.net
Comprehensive site that also includes free e-mail newsletters.

Information Technology Professional's Resource Center
www.itprc.com
This site lists on-line data networking resources.

InformationWeek.com
www.informationweek.com
On-line component of *Information Week* magazine.

IT papers.com
www.ITpapers.com
Site includes thousands of articles on IT subjects for reference.

The New York Times On-line
www.nytimes.com
On-line version of the publication.

Profnet
www.profnet.com
Search the on-line database or submit a query to find experts in particular areas; you can also sign up for free e-mail releases about new research and story ideas.

techtarget.com
http://whatis.techtarget.com
On-line encyclopedia of IT-related terms.

TechWeb
www.techweb.com
Reports on tech news; includes e-mail newsletters, along with an
encyclopedia of IT terms.

Wall Street Journal On-line
www.wsj.com
On-line version of the publication.

Wired News
www.wired.com
On-line version of *Wired* magazine.

ZDNet
www.zdnet.com
Another source for tech news.

IT Consulting and Advisory Firms

Some of the major firms include:

Aberdeen Group
www.aberdeen.com
IT market analysis and consulting firm; provides sources for
articles.

AMR Research
www.amrresearch.com
IT market analysis and consulting firm; provides sources for
articles.

Forrester Research
www.forrester.com
IT research and consulting firm; provides sources for articles.

Gartner Group
www4.gartner.com
IT research and consulting firm; provides analysts and sources for articles.

Giga Information Group
www.gigaweb.com
IT advisory firm; provides analysts for articles.

IDC
www.idc.com
Provider of technology forecasts, insight, and advice; provides article sources.

META Group
www.metagroup.com
IT research and consulting firm; provides analysts and sources for articles.

Yankee Group
www.yankeegroup.com
IT research and consulting firm; provides sources for articles.

Other Associations/Organizations

Computing Technology Industry Association
450 E. 22nd St., Suite 230
Lombard, IL 60148-6158
Phone: 630-268-1818
Fax: 630-268-1384
Web: www.comptia.org

The association consists of more than 10,000 companies and professional IT members in the computing and communications market; serves as an information clearinghouse and resource for the industry.

Independent Computer Consultants Association
11131 S. Towne Square, Suite F
St. Louis, MO 63123
Phone: 314-892-1675 or 800-774-4222
Fax: 314-487-1345
Web: www.icca.org
The association is a national network of independent computer consultants; members objectively support the best computer or software solutions in all areas of the computer industry, from hardware design to systems integration to employee training.

Internet Society
11150 Sunset Hills Road, Suite 100
Reston, VA 20190-9880
Phone: 703-326-9880
Fax: 703-326-9881
Web: www.isoc.org
The Internet Society consists of technologists, developers, educators, researchers, government representatives, and business people; the 9,000-member group seeks to ensure global cooperation coordination for the Internet and related technologies and applications.

US Internet Industry Association
5810 Kingstowne Center Drive
Suite 120, PMB 212
Alexandria, VA 22315-5711
Phone: 703-924-0006
Fax: 703-924-4203
This trade association has more than 300 members and provides

them with business news, information, and support relating to Internet commerce, content, and connectivity.

Writers' Organizations and Other Resources

Society for Technical Communication
901 N. Stuart St., Suite 904
Arlington, VA 22203-1822
Phone: 703-522-4114
Fax: 703-522-2075
Web: www.stc.org
The 22,000-member society includes writers, editors, educators, scientists, engineers, artists, and publishers who are professionally engaged in or interested in the field of technical communication.

Books

The Tech Writer's Survival Guide:
A Comprehensive Handbook for Aspiring Technical Writers
by Janet Van Wicklen (Checkmark Books, 2001)
Although aimed at technical writers, the 19 chapters offer some good background information and tips for writing about technological subjects; includes list of professional associations.

Technical Writing for Dummies
by Sheryl Lindsell-Roberts (Hungry Minds, 2001)
This book is also geared for technical writers, but its 22 chapters include useful information, including a rundown of punctuation and grammar rules, abbreviations, and an appendix of technical terms.

CHAPTER 9

The Mommy (or Daddy) Track

Writing About Parenting

The Basics: What You Need to Know

Up to your ears in dirty diapers and carpools? As a parent, you're uniquely qualified to write for one of the largest freelance markets there is. Hundreds of magazines, newspapers, and Web sites are constantly in search of parenting pieces that entertain and inspire as they inform. New and inexperienced writers often break into freelancing by writing about parenting issues, and writers who develop a specialty in this area often find that they need look no further than their own families for story ideas.

But writing about parenting and child care is more than simply relating personal experience—parenting writers are expected to keep up with trends, locate and interview experts, and provide plenty of service for readers. If you're a parent—or if you just want to write about kids and the issues a family faces—this specialty is worth considering.

The Nuts and Bolts:
Writing About Parenting and Child Care

Don't Preach

Ask any new parent and he or she will tell you—when it comes to parenting, everyone has an opinion and no one thinks twice about sharing it with you (like it or not). If the baby cries, pick her up immediately—or she'll be traumatized. Nope, that's the worst thing you can do—you'll spoil her if you don't let her cry herself to sleep. Let him suck on a pacifier and he'll need thousands of dollars' worth of orthodontia . . . or take it away from him too early and he'll need therapy for separation anxiety years later.

While many of these issues are intensely personal, parents face dozens if not hundreds of decisions every day that will affect their children's welfare. What's a mom or dad to do? Most look to parenting or child-care publications for advice, information, and support.

The most important rule in writing about parenting is to avoid preaching or implying that there is only one way to do something. "Parenting is so subjective. Everyone feels differently about how they want to parent, and you don't want to turn people off," says Melanie Bowden, a freelancer in Davis, California. "You want to say, 'This is one option.'

"A typical example is the whole family-bed issue—people get touchy about it and it's really a personal decision. It's the same thing with breastfeeding. When you write about anything like that, you want to give options but also support whatever people decide to do."

Provide Service

When you write about parenting, you're often providing some kind of service to the person reading the article. In fact, how-to articles are the most prevalent kind of parenting stories and for good reason.

"Parents are busy and they want you to get to the point," says Kathy Sena, a freelancer in Manhattan Beach, California. "They want practical, real-world tips. They love sidebars, boxes, and bullets, and so do parenting magazines. Parents want to hear from experts, and a little theory is fine—but get to the point quickly and show them how they can use what you're telling them."

Find Supporting Experts

Okay, so you're a parent—a good parent, possibly even a great parent. But it takes more than that to write with authority about parenting and child care. "Just because you're a parent, don't assume you're an expert on parenting," says Lain Ehmann, a freelancer in Los Gatos, California. "I think that a lot of people think once they have a kid it's an easy topic to write about. For that very reason, the people who can write about parenting well stand out that much more clearly."

Even if you have personal experience with an issue, you'll need to back up the advice you offer with expert opinions and quotes. "You still need the experts, the research, and the writing skills like in any other field," says Ehmann. You may have to interview pediatricians, child-development experts, dieticians, or teachers, in addition to including real-life anecdotes. And in most cases, you won't want to rely on your child's doctor as an expert—editors prefer someone who is established or well-known in his or her field. Call organizations like the American Medical Association or the American Dietetic Association and ask for referrals to members who specialize in the area you're writing about.

Create Your Own Web Presence

I set up a Web site. It took a lot of time to set up initially, but now when someone wants clips I just point them there.

It is so much easier than sending/putting together packets after each query.

And I also think that if a site is well-designed, editors are much more likely to spend a little time browsing than they would looking through just another packet of clips.

Color makes a big difference, too. Color copies of your clips are too expensive to mail out in every packet, but you can easily present your work in color on your Web site.

—Ari Tye Radetsky, Denver, Colorado

Write for the Audience

Remember that parents come in all ages, both sexes, and are of every race, ethnicity, and religion. This may seem obvious but too often writers simply assume that their family traditions—such as celebrating Christmas—are embraced by all readers. "Unless a magazine has a very specific audience, you're going to have to appeal to a wide range of parents," says Ehmann. "You've got stay-at-home moms, working moms, stay-at-home dads, working dads, two-mother couples, two-father couples, Christian, Jewish, you name it. Parenting cuts across all that, and you have to be mindful of that as you're writing because it's very easy to offend people in the parenting realm."

On the other hand, if you're writing for a publication aimed at a more narrow audience—say, stay-at-home mothers or parents who home-school their children—it's okay to focus your story on that group of people. Just keep the audience in mind as you write the piece.

Consider Regional Publications

While many writers aspire to be published in national parenting magazines like *Child*, *Parents*, and *Parenting*, there are hundreds of regional parenting and child-care publications as well. The vast majority of them need and use freelance material. The rates aren't high, but these markets are a good place for new freelancers to get assignments and clips—and offer reprint possibilities as well. Keep in mind, though, that the editors are often overworked and understaffed. "When you're talking about small regional publications, you have to be really patient in terms of them getting back to you," says Bowden.

Regional publications may also want you to use local experts and sources for articles; make sure you know what the editor wants before you start the story. "For local publications, look and see what types of stories they run. If they have something they run every year at the same time, offer to write it—because the staffers are sick of writing it," suggests Bowden. "For example, some magazines run stories every summer on things to do with your kids, or round-ups of local camps. And people on staff are tired of doing that. It is a grind, but it can get you into the magazine."

Look Beyond Your Own Experience

No doubt your own children or grandchildren will provide you with fodder for story ideas. But don't neglect articles aimed at other ages as well. While there's a bigger market for stories aimed at parents of infants to school-aged children than for the parents of teenagers, you don't want to pigeonhole yourself by writing only about babies simply because you have a new one at home.

"Look beyond your own kids for ideas and anecdotes for your stories," agrees Ehmann. "I can be really narrow-sighted because I have younger kids—so I tend to focus on younger kids. Yet the scope of any given publication may be ages 3 to 12, so you need to go beyond your own immediate experiences."

But Don't Be Afraid to Share

At the same time, though, your firsthand examples can enrich your writing. Readers may find it easier to relate to someone who's "been there."

"I've found that the specific is universal in parenting writing—and probably in all writing," says Sena. "For example, when I wrote about the problems I had with breastfeeding when my son was born, I got into the nitty-gritty details of my specific situation. But I received many e-mails saying things like 'that's exactly what I went through!'"

Your parenting experience is an important part of the equation when it comes to writing about it, says Leah Ingram, a freelancer in New Hope, Pennsylvania. "When I was working as an editor of a now-defunct parenting magazine, I did assign stories to people who didn't have kids. But I tended to favor those writers who could bring personal experience to their stories, such as their own parenting anecdotes," says Ingram. "In addition, parents who are writers often ask insightful questions of experts that a nonparent wouldn't even think to consider."

Include Anecdotes

Because there are so many different approaches to parenting, readers like hearing about more than one person's experience or opinion in child-care articles. A wide range of sources helps ensure that readers will find something in an article that benefits them.

"Advice varies greatly, especially when it comes to parenting," says Diane Benson Harrington, a freelancer in Moline, Illinois. "Since every child is unique, I think it's important to give parents more than one way to solve a problem or look at an issue. I also like to interview more than one expert (I talk to a minimum of three, plus parents themselves, for nearly every story) because I like to make sure the advice is sound. If two or more people sing the same tune, that provides a sounder basis for the idea."

Create New Spins on Evergreen Topics

Many parenting stories cover topics like health, child development, discipline, and nutrition. While these subjects are covered over and over again, look for a new angle or new approach to sell your story idea. "Because it's happening for the first time to you, you think it's a new fresh idea. That's not always the truth," says Ehmann.

"Although parenting publications tend to repeat a lot of the same issues, they want a new take on it. For example, just because you're going through the 'should I work, should I stay home?' debate, the publications have probably been through that—up, down, sideways, and back and forth—so you need to think of a new spin on it."

Although you may need to come up with a fresh approach, parenting writers have an endless list of "evergreen" story ideas to choose from. Topics include infant first aid, children's health, how to choose a babysitter, how to help kids prepare for and succeed in school, discipline strategies, inexpensive craft activities, proper nutrition, ways to talk to kids about difficult subjects . . . the list goes on and on. The trick is coming up with a new or unique angle.

"Parenting is a never-ending subject," agrees Bowden. "Stories about health and development are popular. Discipline is a big topic, as are helping kids do well in school, socializing, personality traits, dealing with bullies, things like that. Parenting magazines are also really big on seasonal stuff, especially back-to-school issues. They'll run things in October about how to make a Halloween costume, for example, and they're always looking for stuff on Christmas and holidays."

Offer Reprint Rights

Many parenting writers maximize their income by selling reprint rights to a variety of regional publications. Melanie Bowden maintains a database of regional publications for this purpose. "Sometimes I'll sell an article to a local publication, and then I'll do a huge e-mail to my huge database, offering it as a reprint. You've already written it, and it's not much more work except for putting a letter together," she says. "Most small regionals are open to that—they're not that picky because they need content. I get anywhere from $30 to $75 or $80 for a regional reprint."

Sena also developed a network of regional publications for her parenting and health stories, and resells most of the articles

Sell More Reprints

Reprints are the best way to increase income.

Two things I do to sell more reprints: (1) I think ahead when pitching new stories—is this something I'll be able to sell elsewhere? How much tweaking might it need to resell?

(2) Once a week, I spend an hour tracking down possible new reprint markets and sending them my clip list and resume.

I've now developed quite a list. I keep a running file on any publication that shows the slightest interest, and I check back with them regularly. Keeping in regular contact makes for lots of sales.

Plus, if they get pinched for an article at deadline time, they know they can call me and I can send something immediately.

—Nicole Burnham Onsi, Hopkinton, Massachusetts

she writes. "About 40 percent of my income comes from reprints," says Sena. "The checks aren't that big—maybe $50 or $75 a story—but they add up quickly!"

Tales from the Front: Diane Benson Harrington

Diane Benson Harrington has been writing since she was 12, and freelancing full-time since 1989. Harrington, who lives in Moline, Illinois, had written a few parenting articles before she became a mom herself, but then cracked markets like *Parents* and *Parenting* once she had children of her own.

In the past several years, she's covered a variety of parenting and child-care subjects, and has taught query-writing classes as well. She offers the following tips for writers who want to break into this field:

- *Do use anecdotes.* Nothing makes a story more appealing and easier to relate to than real-life examples of what kids or parents have done or experienced.

- *Do talk to more than one or two people.* You want to corroborate any advice you're providing (because, depending on the topic, the wrong advice could be harmful to a child). Plus, interviewing a well-chosen handful of people makes a story more comprehensive and gives you better information to draw from.

- *Do use conversational writing.* Write like you're talking to a friend, so the story will be easy to read. Be sure to use a confident tone, too, so readers feel confident that this "friend" knows what she's talking about.

- *Do come up with fresh twists on old topics.* Parenting magazines recycle story topics all the time, out of necessity. (Parents always want to read about potty-training, discipline, behavior, education, etc.) For example, instead of an article on general childproofing, Harrington pitched an article called "Childproofing: The Advanced Class," about how parents can get lax on safety issues when their children reach the age of five—and what parents still need to be vigilant about. Similarly, instead of a bland article on preparing kids for school, she pitched "What Teachers Wish Parents Knew."

- *Don't write in long, wordy sentences.* Parents are pressed for time. Bullet points and subheadings make for easier, faster reading—and these techniques also help you organize your story.

- *Don't assume there is only one answer to every problem.* The one-size-fits-all approach to parenting is misguided and leaves plenty of readers feeling left out.

The Markets: Where to Sell Your Work

Many smaller and regional markets for parenting articles may not be listed in publications like *The Writer's Handbook* or *Writer's Market.* While national magazines pay more than $1 per word for parenting articles, the regional markets, Web sites, and newspapers offer varying rates.

Some of the biggest markets for parenting-related writing include:

- *National parenting magazines*—these glossy markets cover nearly every aspect of parenting and child care, including children's health, nutrition, development, childhood diseases, first aid, and preventive medicine; rates are high, but these magazines can be difficult to break into.

- *Regional parenting magazines and publications*—many writers start with these publications, as there is less competition than at the national glossies. Coverage area depends on the publication, but many focus on local events, activities, and resources.

- *Women's and men's magazines*—these magazines, particularly women's publications, often include parenting and child-care subjects, either in a regular section of the magazine or as features. Stories range from typical service pieces to features, essays, and family travel.

- *General interest magazines*—the markets may cover trends in parenting, new research, children's health, and other related topics.

- *Parenting-oriented Web sites*—these markets cover a variety of child-care topics. As with other on-line publications, stories tend to run shorter than in print markets and include quizzes, links to other sites, and other interactive features.

- *National/major newspapers*—cover parenting and family issues; often have a section devoted to family life.

- *Regional/city general interest magazines and newspapers*—like their national counterparts, regional and city publications also often include parenting and child-care subjects.

Other Useful Stuff

Often, when writing about parenting, you'll have a need to find qualified experts. Some possible sources are given below, along with other associations that may be helpful:

Associations/Organizations

American Academy of Pediatrics
141 Northwest Point Boulevard
Elk Grove Village, IL 60007-1098
Phone: 847-434-4000
Fax: 847-434-8000
Web: www.aap.org

This 55,000-member organization consists of pediatricians and pediatric subspecialties.

American Dietetic Association (ADA)
216 W. Jackson Boulevard
Chicago, IL 60606-6995
Phone: 312-899-0040
Fax: 312-899-1979
Web: http://eatright.org
This 64,000-member organization is made up of registered dietitians, dietetic technicians, and other professionals. The ADA promotes nutrition, health, and well-being and publishes *The Journal of the American Dietetic Association*; also offers nutritional and statistical information to journalists and references to ADA spokespersons for expert sources.

American Medical Association
515 N. State St.
Chicago, IL 60610
Phone: 312-464-5000
Fax: 312-464-4184
Web: www.ama-assn.org
The AMA is the largest medical organization in the country, with 297,000 medical doctors. The AMA publishes *The Journal of the American Medical Association* and disseminates scientific information to members and the public.

American Pediatric Society
3400 Research Forest Drive, Suite B7
The Woodlands, TX 77381-4259
Phone: 281-419-0052
Fax: 281-419-0082
Web: www.aps-spr.org
This society consists of M.D. educators and researchers who are

interested in the study of childhood diseases, prevention of illness, and promotion of children's health.

Center for the Improvement of Child Caring
11331 Ventura Blvd., Suite 103
Studio City, CA 91604-3147
Phone: 818-980-0903 or 800-325-2422
Fax: 818-753-1054
Web: http://www.ciccparenting.org
With 1,000 members, this organization supports instructors and groups involved in delivering parenting education services.

National Parenting Association
51 W. 74th St., Suite 1B
New York, NY 10023
Phone: 212-362-7575 or 800-709-8795
Fax: 212-362-1916
Web: http://parentsunite.org
This 7,000-member organization of parents serves as a think-tank to identify and consider economic, social, and political issues important to parents; conducts polls, and surveys.

National Parents Association (NPA)
603 E. Lincoln Way Ave.
Valparaiso, IN 46383
Phone: 219-462-9996
Fax: 219-464-3583
This is a 5,000-member organization of parents interested in sharing ideas on raising children; the group conducts educational programs and publishes a bimonthly newsletter.

National PTA/National Congress of Parents and Teachers
330 N. Wabash Ave., Suite 2100
Chicago, IL 60610-3690
Phone: 312-670-6782 or 800-307-4PTA

Fax: 312-670-6783
Web: www.pta.org
This 6,500,000-member organization consists of parents, teachers, students, principals, and administrators, and has a core staff of 60 people; its mission is to promote children's welfare and encourage parent involvement in public schools.

Parents Helping Parents (PHP)
3041 Olcott St.
Santa Clara, CA 95054-3222
Phone: 408-727-5775
Fax: 408-727-0182
Web: http://www.php.com
With a membership of 19,000, this organization helps children with special needs receive care, services, education, and acceptance.

Parents Without Partners (PWP)
1650 S. Dixie Highway, Suite 510
Boca Raton, FL 33432
Phone: 561-391-8833 or 800-637-7974
Fax: 561-395-8557
Web: www.parentswithoutpartners.org
This 45,000-member organization aims to alleviate the problems of single parents in relation to the welfare and upbringing of their children.

Other Resources for Writers

Profnet
www.profnet.com
Search the on-line database or submit a query to find experts in particular areas; you can also sign up for free e-mail releases about new research and story ideas.

Parenting Publications of America (PPA)
5820 Wilshire Blvd., Suite 500
Los Angeles, CA 90036-4500
Phone: 323-937-5514
Fax: 210-348-8397
Web: www.parentingpublications.org
E-mail: parpubs@family.com
Consisting of mostly regional parenting publications, this organization promotes publications for and about parents and compiles statistics. PPS is also a source for possible reprint markets as well.

CHAPTER 10

Taking a Trip

Writing About Travel

The Basics: What You Need to Know

There's an ongoing interest in travel, whether to local, inexpensive family attractions or high-budget adventures on the other side of the world. While well-paid full-time travel journalists are somewhat rare, there are many markets for the writer who wants to include travel stories in his or her repertoire.

How do travel writers turn their vacations into high-paying article assignments? What kinds of markets are interested in travel stories? How you can break into this popular area?

The following pages reveal how you can turn your travels—whether they're close to home or thousands of miles away—into an income-producing sideline.

The Nuts and Bolts:
How to Write About Travel

Breaking In

Travel writing can be a difficult specialty to get into, in part because so many journalists are eager to enter the field. (Isn't it obvious why? Write about travel, and you can start writing off your trips and vacations—as business expenses!) While some travel writers start out as freelancers writing about travel, most get into this area after they've already established themselves writing about other specialties.

Using your current contacts to nail your first travel writing assignments is one of the easiest ways to get your foot in the door. That's how Leslie Gilbert Elman of New York, New York, got her first travel piece.

"I had been writing women's service features for a magazine that also ran travel stories," says Elman. "The editor and I had a solid, long-standing relationship. One month, she needed someone to write a travel piece and she assigned it to me. It was something of a perk, since she knew and liked me. That gave me my first bona fide 'destination' story."

But afterwards, Elman found it difficult to obtain additional assignments. She decided to write some pieces for newspapers on spec to obtain clips and build her portfolio. "One of them sold to *The Dallas Morning News*. In a way, that sale was the most satisfying because it was made on a totally blind query," says Elman. "The travel editor wasn't someone I knew. She didn't have to buy the piece, but she did. That gave me confidence."

Be Ready to Work

Perhaps no other nonfiction writing field produces such an image of glamour as travel writing. A travel writer lolls about on a pristine white beach, an exotic rum drink in one hand, jotting a few notes about a luxurious all-expenses-paid trip for a thousand-dollar payoff.

Yeah, right. Ask any travel writer, and she'll tell you the reality is far removed from this idyllic image.

"Travel writing is not a vacation. If you're doing it right, you're working hard day and night," says Elman. "You're interviewing all sorts of people, from hotel managers to locals in the markets. You're shooting photos, taking notes, and juggling a million ideas at any given time."

If the idea of having to "work" during your vacation turns you off, then this field may not be right for you.

"It's easy to abuse the privilege of being a travel writer. There are a lot of 'posers' who enter the field thinking that it's a lark," says Elman. "Those people don't last long. Professionals in the industry—writers, editors, and PR people—talk to each other. You have to comport yourself as a professional and maintain a good reputation, or you won't make it."

Don't Quit Your Day Job—Yet

Unlike some other writing specialties—like health, business, and technology—it's more difficult to make a good living writing only travel stories. As a result, most writers cover other areas in addition to travel.

"Travel writing is highly competitive," says Elman. "It is very hard to sell stories and establish relationships with reputable publications. It's really not an area for beginners."

Many travel writers have developed complementary specialties. They may write about travel and business, for example—or travel and food, or travel and sports. "I've never just gone and done a travel story," says Tim Harper, a freelancer in Ridgewood, New Jersey, who's written dozens of travel articles.

"What I've done is tied together travel stories with other stories. Let's say a magazine sends me someplace to do a feature.

Drop a Name

Work an "in" any way you can. If I've been referred by a mutual friend, I'll write "referred by ___" on the bottom left corner of my envelope. And I'll mention it in the first line of my query letter.

That blurb on the envelope has earned my proposals a bit better treatment and quicker response than the rest of them in the stack.

—Kristin Baird Rattini, Shanghai, China

I'll try to bring them more than they asked me to do. I'll come back and say, 'You sent me to Sweden to do this business story on the Swedish economy, but I also have this nice little travel story on Sweden in winter—would you like that?'

"A lot of times they'll buy it," says Harper. "But if not, I've offered it to them and can then sell it elsewhere."

The Ethics

One of the hottest issues facing travel writers is the question of whether to accept "comps," or complimentary trips. Writers and editors may be invited on all-expenses-paid, fact-finding trips sponsored by local or national tourist offices, tour organizers, resorts, airlines, or other companies. Some publications prohibit travel writers from accepting this kind of subsidized travel because editors believe they can influence a writer's objectivity.

Should you accept comps? The bottom line is that it may be impossible to make a living writing about travel if you don't, say many experienced travel writers. And most journalists wind up covering more than one story on such trips to maximize their income. "Most of the travel-writing industry depends on some overlap, and to some degree on subsidized travel," says freelancer Tom Brosnahan of Concord, Massachusetts, who's authored more than 35 books and 100 articles on travel. "You don't go for one article—you can't."

"You can repurpose the material," agrees JoAnn Milivojevic, a freelancer in Chicago who specializes in travel. "It's more fun, too. I try to think of how many ways I can slice and dice the information and who would be interested in it."

Know Your Subject

With other types of writing—say parenting or health—you can usually research a story through telephone interviews and by reading background material, studies, and the like. With travel, there's simply no substitute for knowing the destination you're covering, whether you're writing a guidebook or a service-related travel story. "If you really know what you're talking about, the reader can sense the depth that comes through," says Brosnahan. "You want a sense of background in your writing."

You can provide this sense of background by including concrete details—like converting the price of a cheap dinner to American dollars. When you're traveling, make notes of your surroundings so that you can incorporate them later on.

And don't just rely on your eyes—use all five senses. What does the market smell like? What sounds do you hear as you wake up in the morning? What flavors does the local cuisine feature? Keeping a travel diary will help you recall these kinds of specifics.

"It's really what you see, what you smell, what you hear, and what you taste that sets the place apart," says Milivojevic. "And have conversations with people. It's really important to talk to everyone from the cab driver and the store owner to the other higher officials you might have access to. Talking to the guy or gal on the corner—that's how you find out what a place is really like."

Think Service

Some travel stories simply tell a story about a person's journey. When writing service-related travel articles, though, you want to deliver as much relevant information about the destination as possible. That doesn't mean your stories should read like business memos or be limited to a list of phone numbers, prices, and travel tips.

Find your voice and write creatively, and you'll be more likely to sell your work. "For magazine writing to be successful, you have to try to get 110 percent into the article," says Brosnahan. "All the service stuff *plus* enough of your personality to really build your reputation. That is what is going to differentiate you from other writers—you have to be kind of stylish."

While you want to communicate with your readers, you can and usually should put something of yourself into the story. "Write about something you've done. The stuff that looks and sounds bad is the stuff you've gotten it from secondary sources.

"What people want to read about is the story, and generally that's your story," says Harper. "For example, my story on narrow-boating in England opened with my son falling in the water. That really got us into the whole experience, and what it was like to be on this boat and mooring and having lunch in the canal-side pubs, which were unique in their own way.

"Do something a little different. Think of travel editors as movie critics. They've seen a lot of bad stuff, and they tend to like anything a little different."

Take Photos

While it depends on the market, one of the most effective ways to increase your travel-writing sales is to include photographs with your stories. "Certainly for newspapers, when you can send them a complete package, you're more likely to make the sale," says Milivojevic. "It makes the editor's life easier, and any time you can save them the hassle, you're a better candidate in their minds."

Agreeing to provide photos with travel stories also improves your bottom line. Markets will pay additional for photos, and you may make more on the photos than from the story itself!

If you're an inexperienced photographer, take a class to learn the basics of photography, including what types of film work best in different situations and how to frame shots. Check with the markets to learn how they want photos submitted—whether as color prints, slides, or digital shots.

It's worth a try. Even if you don't sell them, you'll have some great photo memories of your trip.

Gather the Information

Remember that readers are going to rely on and use the information you provide them, so it must be accurate. Double-check data like names, addresses, phone numbers, rates, dates of events, and other relevant information before you turn in the story.

When traveling or researching a story, keep detailed files of any information that you may want to use in the future. Most travel writers come home with sheaths of papers, contacts, notes, and other background that they can then use in the future.

"I'll often take one of those accordion binders with me and separate it into sections for restaurants, lodging, and attractions," says Milivojevic. "Then I grab brochures and magazines and stuff like that and just stuff them into the proper categories. When I get home, everything is there."

Consider the Markets

When writing on travel, consider the markets before you pitch articles. Is the magazine aimed at an affluent audience? Is the focus on adventure travel or on more sedate trips? Targeting your queries will help you get more assignments and spin more than one story out of every trip you take.

"I think that's part of the pitching process. I've gathered all the research and have it all on a plate. Then I look at who my audience is for this material and what they want to know, and then what audience does a particular magazine serve," says Milivojevic.

"So, for example, for a family-oriented magazine, I'm going to want to tell them about the family-oriented activities on the Cayman Islands—and maybe interview a kid or two while I'm at the Turtle Farm.

"If I'm doing a nightlife story for another magazine, that's going to be a completely different spiel. It's going to be sexier,

Note Story Sources

I write the phone number and e-mail address of the editor on the outside of each job folder.

As I interview experts, I add their names and contact information on the outside, too.

That way, I don't have to rifle through a Rolodex or scraps of paper when I need to make a few quick calls—or when the editor asks for numbers for fact-checking.

And if I end up doing a similar or related story, my experts' numbers are all in one place, filed away with the story folder and easily accessible.

—Sharon Miller Cindrich, Wauwatosa, Wisconsin

and more sensual. It's going to be set at night, and be more about the music and cocktails, and that kind of thing."

Look beyond the "typical" markets when pitching travel stories, too. "A travel writer can sell stories to the resort market, regional city magazines, newspapers, business publications, and even political newspapers," says freelancer Jackie Dishner of Phoenix, Arizona, who writes about travel, arts, and entertainment. "You can write travelogues (narratives about your trip), destination pieces (features that tell the reader where to go when visiting a place), shopping stories, food pieces, etc.

"I write shopping stories for one magazine on a regular basis. I write destination pieces occasionally for a political paper. And I'm trying to sell more travelogues to other markets. The more you get your name out there, the more people recognize you and will actually call you to write stories about their cities and venues."

Pitch New Angles

When pitching story ideas, try to come up with new angles on tried-and-true destination stories. Instead of pitching Paris as the city for lovers or "April in Paris," pitch it as a great family destination. Come up with new ideas for fun family vacations, or suggest weekend getaways with a different twist.

Harper concentrates on tightly focused stories rather than general service-oriented ones. "Each story usually has a very sharp narrow angle—like going to Rome with kids or going narrow-boating on the English canal," says Harper. "I don't like to do the whole big encompassing story because they're so hard to sell. Don't try to take some big topic. Instead, pick some narrow little slice of what you're doing that has a specific thing to do that might have general interest. Maybe it's a certain type of museum, a certain walk through the volcanoes, or something that has a bit of a twist to it—one that is pretty specific."

Also, ask markets for their editorial calendars. Many travel magazines plan their issues or predetermine what destinations they'll cover months in advance. By reviewing their guidelines, you can pitch ideas that match their needs, or suggest stories that complement their plans.

Explore the Locale

If you've spent any time traveling, you probably already know that there's a certain amount of sameness in many locations. As a travel writer, your job is to find the details that make a location or experience unique and share them with your reader. In other words, find the details that most effectively describe the experience of being there.

Ask yourself, how is this hotel or restaurant or beach or ski resort or cruise ship different from others that are similar to it? You may have to come up some pretty subtle differences, but keep them in mind as you're traveling and later in writing the piece. This is where paying attention to all five senses and taking detailed notes will help you later. You also have to be willing to explore, and be open to new experiences.

"The people are a big part of it, as is your willingness to go off the beaten path," says Milivojevic. "You have to get out of the resort and go into that small fishing village and hang around and be open and talk to people. What kind of music are they listening to? What kinds of spices do they use for their food? What do they eat? When do they eat? "What's the 'vibe'? Do you feel welcome? Comfortable? Intimidated? All of those come rushing at you if you go off by yourself to a nontourist place."

Tale from the Front: Kathy Landis

Kathy Landis of Orangevale, California, has been writing about travel as a freelancer for 17 years. She started out writing for regional parenting magazines and regional newspapers, and has written for dozens of publications including *American Way*,

US Airways, *Country Living*, *Coastal Living*, and *Country Home*. Her tips for travel writers include the following:

- *Buy a camera and use it.* Photographs increase the value of your travel articles, particularly when you're writing for newspapers. Learn the basics of photography early on.

- *Pitch a travel column to your local newspaper* if it doesn't already have one. Landis began writing a column for a regional newspaper, which led to dozens of clips and opened a lot of doors for her; scouting for ideas also led to stories for other publications.

- *Network.* Attending press trips, meetings, writer's conferences, and other events can lead to great connections and more work. Landis met another writer on a press trip who hooked her up with a guidebook publisher, and she ended up landing a freelance gig from her new connection.

- *Take advantage of travel, convention, and PR people* who represent destinations, historical societies, resorts, and the like. They know the nuts and bolts of their areas; you can call them or visit their Web sites for information. And, after taking a trip, send a published clip to those sources you used; it's always appreciated and keeps your name in front of them.

- *Think of multiple markets for your stories.* Landis has sold a number of articles to more than one publication. For example, she wrote a piece on some local caverns for a local parenting publication. Thereafter she sold it to *Off Road*, a magazine for four-wheel-drive enthusiasts; then she sold it again as a lifestyle piece (featuring a well-known caver) to *US Airways*. She sold it once more (about interesting finds in caves) to *Boy's Life*; and finally sold it to the New York Times syndicate. The story, which originally had earned her $25, has now brought in an additional $3,000 to $4,000.

The Markets: Where to Sell Travel

While regional and national newspapers used to be among the most lucrative markets for travel, most papers are buying fewer travel stories from freelancers. There are still plenty of markets for travel writing, but new writers may have to start at the bottom with small, local publications to get some clips before pitching to the better-paying markets.

Some of the potential markets for travel stories include:

- *Travel-specific magazines*—these publications focus on travel but their audiences vary; *Arthur Frommer's Budget Travel* has a different slant than *Travel & Leisure*, for example.

- *General interest magazines*—most publications include travel stories that may be geared to seasonal topics.

- *Women's and men's magazines*—these magazines often cover travel, usually from a service-oriented angle.

- *Parenting magazines*—these often include travel articles, specifically taking trips with children and to family-friendly destinations.

- *Health and fitness magazines*—cover travel, including destination pieces, spas and resorts, adventure travel, and other related stories.

- *Cooking/food magazines*—these publications often include travel stories, usually with a cooking or food angle.

- *Inflight magazines*—a good market for travel stories; make sure that your destination is one covered by the airline that publishes the magazine.

- *Travel-oriented Web sites*—these sites cover travel; as with other on-line publications, stories tend to run shorter than in print markets, and include quizzes, links to other sites, and other interactive features.

- *National/major newspapers*—most still do buy freelance travel pieces; some want queries while others want the completed manuscript.

- *Regional/city magazines and newspapers*—like their national counterparts, regional and city publications also publish travel stories, often with a local angle.

Other Useful Stuff

When planning a trip or a travel story, contact the local convention and visitor's bureau for information. If you're traveling to an international destination, get in touch with the country's tourism board or other association or agency for background information, statistics, story ideas, and the like.

Other possible resources for travel writers are listed below:

Associations/Organizations

American Hotel and Lodging Association
1201 New York Avenue NW, #600
Washington, D.C. 20005-3931
Phone: 202-289-3100
Fax: 202-289-3199
Web: www.ahma.com
The association provides operations, technical, educational, marketing, and communications services to members; includes a library that is open to the public by appointment.

American Society of Travel Agents
1101 King St., #200
Alexandria, VA 22314-2944
Phone: 703-739-2782
Fax: 703-684-8319
Web: www.astanet.com

The society consists of representatives of the travel agency industry.

International Association of Amusement Parks and Attractions
1448 Duke Street
Alexandria, VA 22314
Phone: 703-836-4800
Fax: 703-836-4801
Web: www.iaapa.org
The association is made up of companies in the amusement parks and attractions industry.

International Association of Convention and Visitor Bureaus
2025 M St. NW, #500
Washington, D.C. 20036-3349
Phone: 202-296-7888
Fax: 202-296-7889
Web: www.iacvb.org
The association consists of travel- and tourism-related businesses, convention and meeting professionals, and tour operators; encourages business travelers and tourists to visit local historic, cultural, and recreational areas.

International Society of Travel and Tourism Educators (ISTTE)
19364 Wood Crest
Harper Woods, MI 48225
Phone: 313-526-0710
Fax: 313-526-0710
Web: http://www.istte.org/
This organization includes 400 members who are teachers, administrators, and researchers employed by institutions offering courses or degrees in travel and tourism fields. Conducts seminars and forums, and promotes the development and exchange of information related to travel and tourism education.

National Business Travel Association
1650 King St., #401
Alexandria, VA 22314
Phone: 703-684-0836
Fax: 703-684-0263
Web: www.nbta.org
The NBTA consists of corporate travel managers and travel service providers.

Profnet
www.profnet.com
Search the on-line database or submit a query to find experts in particular areas; you can also sign up for free e-mail releases about new research and story ideas.

Travel Industry Association of America
1100 New York Avenue NW, #450
Washington, D.C. 20005
Phone: 202-408-8422
Fax: 202-408-1255
Web: www.tia.org
The association consists of business, professional, and trade associations of the travel industry, as well as state and local associations that promote tourism to a specific region or site.

Writers Organizations and Other Resources

International Food, Wine and Travel Writers Association (IFWTWA)
P.O. Box 8249
Calabasas, CA 91372
Phone: 818-999-9952
Fax: 818-347-7545
Web: http://www.ifwtwa.org
Founded in 1956, this 435-member organization consists of

professional food, wine, and travel journalists in 28 countries; travel and hospitality industry organizations are associate members.

Outdoor Writers Association of America (OWAA)
1212 Hickory St., No. 1
Missoula, MT 59801
Phone: 406-728-7434
Fax: 406-728-7445
Web: http://www.owaa.org
Founded in 1927, this 1800-member organization consists of newspaper, magazine, television, and motion-picture writers and photographers who are concerned with outdoor recreation and conservation. Compiles market data for writer members.

Society of American Travel Writers (SATW)
4101 Lake Boone Tr., Suite 201
Raleigh, NC 27607
Phone: 919-787-5181
Fax: 919-787-4916
Web: http://www.satw.org
Founded in 1956, this organization has 1,150 members, including writers, editors, broadcasters, photographers, and public relations representatives. Publishes *Travel Writer* newsletter, which details industry trends; annual membership directory includes specialties and affiliations.

Travel Journalists Guild (TJG)
P.O. Box 10643
Chicago, IL 60610
Phone: 312-664-9279
Fax: 312-664-9701
Founded in 1980, this organization consists of independent travel writers. The purpose of the 75-member organization is to improve working conditions of travel writers and provide travel

opportunities for purpose of research; sponsors four to six research and writing trips a year.

World Federation of Travel Writers and Journalists (FIJET)
c/o Don Bonhaus
One Ballinswood Road
Atlantic Highlands, NJ 07716-1510
Phone: 732-291-2840
Fax: 732-291-9272
Founded in 1954, this 1700-member organization consists of travel journalists; promotes the professional development of members and conducts educational programs.

Books

Travel Writing: A Guide to Research, Writing and Selling
by L. Peat O'Neill (Writer's Digest Books, 1996)
Nine-chapter comprehensive guide that covers travel writing, includes resources.

The Travel Writer's Handbook:
How to Write and Sell Your Own Travel Experiences
by Louise Purwin Zobel (Surrey Books, 1997)
Eighteen chapters cover all aspects of travel writing, including research, pitching, and crafting stories as well as business issues.

CHAPTER 11

Get Off the Couch

Writing About Fitness & Sports

The Basics: What You Need to Know

Can you tell your traps from your tris? Are you the first at your gym to sign up for a new cardio class? Is fitness an important part of your life? If it is, you already know that fitness is no longer merely a component of health. In fact, there are now entire magazines devoted to fitness aimed at women, men, children, older Americans, and even young mothers-to-be. Most general interest magazines also feature fitness-related articles of some form in every issue.

In addition to straightforward fitness writing, most spectator and participatory sports have at least one magazine—usually many more—for enthusiasts. Local and regional publications are also often searching for talented sportswriters to cover events. If you're a sports buff, writing about this field can enable you to develop a specialty about something you love—and give you an insider's look into the sport, the players, and the coaches as well. Read on to learn how to turn your interest in sports or fitness into a writing niche.

The Nuts and Bolts: How to Write About Fitness and Sports

Know Your Subject

If you're the world's biggest "super-fan," you've got a leg up when it comes to writing about this field. The key to writing about sports is knowing about them. Just ask freelancer Debbie Elicksen who covers hockey from Calgary, Alberta, and has turned a lifelong love affair with hockey into a full-time career.

"Since I was a kid, I pretty much was consumed by hockey and lived, breathed, and ate it," says Elicksen. "Even when I was 11, I was confident that I knew more about hockey than most people in the business. If you don't know about it, research the hell out of it and pretend like you do."

When Elicksen accepted a position as PR director for the Edmonton Trappers, a baseball team, she didn't know much about baseball, but she learned quickly. "Before I went to Edmonton, I probably took every single book that was available and read it from front to cover," she says. "I became an expert in baseball within the span of two weeks."

Chuck Bednar, a freelancer from Wintersville, Ohio, agrees that a solid background is paramount. "First of all, know something about the sport you intend to cover," says Bednar. "You don't need to be an expert but you do need to understand what you're seeing." If you don't understand the rules of the game or the nuances of the sport, it will be impossible to communicate with your readers regardless of the sport you're covering.

Start Off Small

You say you want to write for *Sports Illustrated?* That's great, but you'll probably have to start at the bottom and build your clips before you nail an assignment from one of the major sports publications. "Don't even think about trying for the major markets like *ESPN* and *Sports Illustrated* until you're well-established," says Bednar.

"It's a sad but true fact that these markets are a lot tougher to crack than most people believe. Likewise, drop the pretense that you can talk to a Barry Bonds or a Michael Jordan right off the bat."

Instead, set your sights on smaller publications when you're starting out. Bednar suggests that freelancers break in by contacting their local paper to see if the sports editor needs any correspondents or "stringers" to cover sports events.

When you approach national magazines, consider pitching unique stories that they don't have access to. "Look around your community for local success stories and stories of people overcoming the odds—things a national audience would be interested in but wouldn't be exposed to if you didn't write it," says Bednar, who started covering sports in high school and college for student newspapers. By the time he was in college, he was writing for the local paper and racking up clips.

Develop a Network of Sources

Sports writing can be a very difficult industry to get into. It takes a while for writers to gain credibility. "The tendency seems to be to gravitate toward the people who have been there for a while. That's how I helped myself when I got started—I pretty much got to know everybody in the industry while I was in it," says Elicksen.

Elicksen made a point of befriending scouts, security guards, dressing-room attendants, and team employees when she first started writing about hockey, and her efforts have paid off.

"I tried to get in tight, and some are now very good friends of mine," she says. "The more people you get to know, the more you know what's going on. And again, the more you know about the industry, and the more you learn about the industry, the easier it is to write."

When interviewing athletes, it's important that you know more that just an athlete's latest accomplishment or commercial appearance. Familiarize yourself with his or her statistics and career history and memorize a few of the lesser-known facts to mention in the interview, suggests Cindy BeMent, a freelancer in Warsaw, Indiana, who writes about fitness.

"For example, you could ask something like, 'Even though this is your first professional marathon, you ran the New York City Marathon on a dare when you were eighteen. Tell me more about that,'" says BeMent. "These facts are harder to find, but if you dig, you can come up with them, and they can make for a more colorful interview session.

"Also, get to know some of the lingo of the sport, but don't stretch beyond your comfort level in using it in an interview, lest you make yourself look less knowledgeable."

Keep Your Finger on the Pulse

When you're writing about sports and fitness, you also have to keep up on what's happening. Keep in touch with your network of sources. Track the latest trends. In the fitness world, for instance, yoga, Pilates, and group classes like spinning were immensely popular in the late 1990s, while currently there's a big emphasis on mind-body fitness, weight training, and balanced workout programs.

When covering your favorite sports teams, ask to be included on their media and fan lists; you can track what's happening and come up with new story ideas that way. For example, Elicksen receives regular e-mail and fax updates from the Edmonton Flames and subscribes to *The Hockey News.* If writing about general fitness, trade associations like IDEA and the Aerobic and Fitness Association of America can help you keep abreast of new trends and training ideas.

Use Your Background

You needn't be an aerobics instructor to write fitness-related articles, but being a marathoner or weekend warrior certainly doesn't hurt. Cindy BeMent used her fitness background—she's a certified personal trainer and competitive runner—to enter the freelancing world. While she'd done some sports writing in college, throughout her career she had focused in sales and marketing. When she started freelancing, however, she found that her running background and fitness experience gave her "a leg up" over other writers.

"Writing about running and fitness was a natural entrée into freelancing for me," says BeMent. "I get a steady stream of ideas coming my way from questions, problems, and successes my running students encounter. Plus, I run for sport, so I know the lingo and the proper channels to go through to get access to the pros. That combination made me attractive to editors, even though I didn't have a stack of clips in the beginning."

Follow Your Heart (and Your Heart Rate)

Another key to writing about sports and fitness is to find an area that you enjoy. "Definitely find an area of sports and fitness that you are interested in yourself," says BeMent. "There's always the 'write what you know,' but I don't mean that. I mean write what you are very curious about."

"'Write what you know' is a standard," agrees Tom Bedell, who writes about golf, travel, and beer from Williamsville, Vermont. "Instead, write what you know about or would like to know about." Bedell started writing about golf in the mid-1990s, when he says he realized that the only way to play as much as he wanted was to start writing about it as well. He's successfully created a niche for himself and enjoys covering a variety of golf-related subjects like golf-course architecture for regional and national publications.

Consider the Playing Fields

Whether you're writing about sports or fitness, you'll want to keep the market in mind when pitching story ideas. Consider women's magazines. While nearly everyone runs fitness-related articles, mainstream publications like *Family Circle* and *Woman's Day* tend to feature walking workouts or simpler exercises, while magazines like *Self*, *Shape*, and *Fitness* offer more cutting-edge and complex regimes.

Because of that, it's smart to study the fitness and sports markets you want to write for before you query. How are the articles structured? How broad is the coverage area? What kinds of experts are featured? By getting a good feel for what the markets are looking for, you'll increase your chances of getting an assignment.

"When writing about fitness, think helpful, fresh, and 'different,'" says BeMent. "Really work to find new research and experts with credible backgrounds to help inform your articles. That said, don't be afraid of revisiting a basic topic. As with any good habits we hope to form in life, fitness writing can sometimes serve to refresh and remind its audience about sound principles and safe practices. See if there is a new angle to an old topic, or further studies that could update a particular standard subject."

Stretch Yourself

Many savvy sports and fitness writers eventually expand their niches and begin covering other areas as well. Writing about sports and travel is a natural combination, as is using your fitness background to branch into health or nutrition. "You can write about sports for a while, and if you're a savvy enough marketer, you can segue into some other things," says BeMent.

"I started more on the running end and sport, and then I had to get some more general health clips. One way to steer myself that way was to write about running—and then write about related items like injury prevention and nutrition for that running publication. That way you can kind of bounce over into other stuff."

Get Your Name Out

As mentioned, when you're starting out and you're short on fitness or sports clips, consider pitching to local or regional publications. Bedell wrote his first golf article for a statewide magazine, *Vermont Golf*, and then nailed additional assignments for other regional publications like *New York Golf* and *New Hampshire Golf*, produced by the same publisher. He then leap-frogged to in-flights and travel magazines.

You can also create visibility for yourself and develop clips by writing a sports or fitness column for a local or regional publication, says Bedell, who is the golf columnist for his local daily newspaper. "It doesn't pay much but it's local and I probably get more feedback than from anything else I do," says Bedell.

"And there's a bit of synergy in everything we do. What I write for local paper sometimes becomes research for a larger story. And it helped me learn more about what was becoming my specialty, which was golf."

Tales from the Front: Claire Walter

Claire Walter of Boulder, Colorado, was a magazine editor at *Ski* and worked in public relations, handling ski accounts, before she began freelancing in 1970s. Covering skiing—and eventually

Network with Other Writers

To me, networking is absolutely invaluable.

By talking with other writers, you learn about the pay that you can get that maybe you're not getting now. You learn about new markets, about editorial changes.

And you can get referred to editors you may have otherwise not encountered.

Other writers can offer you an introduction to an editor you might want to work with.

That's been one of my main ways of pitching to new editors, to have a name that I can drop in the first sentence.

That's led to assignments and to relationships that I think are going to last a long time.

—Bob Bittner, Charlotte, Michigan

other sports—was a natural specialty for her. Since then, she has branched out and also writes about food and travel as well. She's the author of hundreds of magazine articles and four books, including *The Complete Idiot's Guide to Fitness* (Alpha Books, 2000).

She offers this advice for writers who want to write about fitness or sports:

- *Walk the walk.* You need to participate in the activity, unless you're writing about something like pro hockey or pro football. Otherwise, when you're writing about something that is a participatory activity, you may miss some obvious aspects of the sport. "I think that's one of the real no-nos," says Walter. "You kind of miss the flavor of what people really do and are concerned about, and what it is like. For example, I wouldn't dream about writing about golf, because I don't golf."

- *Keep up to date.* It's important to stay up on what's happening in the area you cover. Subscribing to trade magazines or other publications geared to people in the business of what you cover can help you pick up on trends and determine whether you're writing about activities that are gaining popularity and gathering interest—or not. Attend trade shows, if you can, and keep up with what people in the industry are reading. "If you are plugged into the industry, whatever it is, and you pick up on these trends, you might be the first person to write about the trend," says Walter, who wrote *Snowshoeing Colorado* (Fulcrum, 1998) after realizing how popular the sport had become. "If I had not been paying attention to that fact, someone else would have written that book."

- *Network.* Join writers' organizations like the American Society of Journalists and Authors (ASJA) and any specialized organizations in your field. "If you're writing about hunting and fishing, join the Outdoor Writers," says Walter. "If you're writing about travel, join the Travel Journalists Guild or the Society of Travel Writers. If you're writing about skiing and snow sports like I am, join the North American Snow Sports Journalism Association." Membership in these organizations keeps you in the loop and can lead to assignments as well.

- *Invest in yourself.* "When people start freelancing, they're often pennywise and pound foolish," says Walter. "People will buy the cheapest stationery and buy crummy business cards, things that don't make them look professional enough to command a decent fee." Spend the money for quality supplies, and present yourself as a professional—and you'll be treated like one.

The Markets: Where to Sell Fitness and Sports

There's no shortage of markets for fitness and sports-related stories, but pay rates vary widely. While national magazines will pay $1/word and up for fitness features and sports articles, smaller and more specialized magazines and markets may pay much less. Near the bottom of the pile are the newspapers; your local paper may pay only $25 to $50 for a sports feature, but these clips can be invaluable when you're entering this field.

Some of the biggest markets for fitness and sports-related writing and their areas of interest include:

- *Fitness magazines*—there are a wide variety of magazines, both national and regional, dedicated to covering fitness topics as well as health, nutrition, and lifestyle subjects.

- *Sports magazines*—nearly every sport has several magazines aimed specifically at fans, participants, and devotees. While these publications have a narrow range of interest, they can offer an opportunity for newer freelancers to break in.

- *General interest magazines*—these often cover fitness and sports topics, whether it is the latest fitness trend or a profile of a famous athlete or sports team.

- *Professional and trade journals*—trade journals for fitness professionals, health-club owners, athletic trainers, and other related medical specialties all offer many opportunities for writers working in this field.

- *Women's and men's magazines*—these magazines cover a broad range of fitness- and sports-related subjects, mostly service-oriented. Both types of magazines include general fitness pieces as well as workout stories; men's magazines may also include sports profiles and other sports-related subjects.

- *Parenting magazines*—cover children's fitness and well-being, and youth sports, as part of covering children's health in general.

- *Cooking/food magazines*—many magazines also cover fitness-related subjects, often focusing on service.

- *Fitness-related and sports Web sites*—while some markets cover a variety of fitness topics, others may limit themselves to addressing a specific sport. As with other on-line publications, stories tend to run shorter than in print markets and include quizzes, links to other sites, and fun interactive features.

- *National/major newspapers*—cover fitness topics as well as sports.

- *Regional/city magazines and newspapers*—like their national counterparts, regional and city publications also cover a broad range of fitness-related topics, often with a regional angle, as well as local sports.

Other Useful Stuff

So, how do you find experts for a fitness story, or locate an association of writers who cover a particular sport? Some useful organizations and resources are listed below:

On-line Resources

InteliHealth
www.intelihealth.com
Offers free e-mail newsletters on a variety of fitness-related topics; Web site also includes basic fitness information.

Newswise
http://www.newswise.com
Newswise offers free e-mail newletters on fitness-related subjects, maintains press releases and an on-line directory of experts.

Profnet
www.profnet.com
Search the on-line database or submit a query to find experts in particular areas; you can also sign up for free e-mail releases about new research and story ideas.

PubMed
http://www.ncbi.nlm.nih.gov/PubMed/
PubMed provides on-line access to the National Library of Medicine, which includes fitness-related research articles.

Reuters Health
http://www.reutershealth.com/
Site that includes daily news releases about fitness, health, and nutrition.

Reward Yourself

To be more productive, I really reward myself and celebrate small victories.

So if I'm struggling with something, I'll play some games with myself—like "I need to write 300 words in the next hour and then I'll call a friend."

It's not huge stuff but it gives me motivation and reminds me of what I love about this job.

—Polly Campbell, Beaverton, Oregon

Associations/Organizations

Aerobic and Fitness Association of America
15250 Ventura Blvd., Suite 200
Sherman Oaks, CA 91403
Phone: 818-905-0040 or 800-446-AFAA
Fax: 818-990-5468
Web: www.afaa.org
This 145,000-member association promotes safety and excellence in exercise instruction; provides certification in aerobics, personal training, and other fitness specialties.

American College of Sports Medicine
401 W. Michigan St.
Indianapolis, IN 46202-3233
Phone: 317-637-9200
Fax: 317-634-7817
Web: www.acsm.org
This 17,500-member organization integrates scientific research, education, and practical applications of sports medicine and exercise science to maintain and improve physical performance, fitness, health, and quality of life. The ACSM also certifies fitness and exercise specialists and instructors.

American Running Association
4405 East-West Highway, Suite 405
Bethesda, MD 20814
Phone: 301-913-9517 or 800-776-ARFA
Fax: 301-913-9520
Web: www.americanrunning.org
This 15,000-member organization consists of runners, exercise enthusiasts, and sports medicine professionals. It promotes running and other aerobic activities and maintains a speakers' bureau.

Cooper Institute for Aerobic Research
12330 Preston Road
Dallas, TX 75230
Phone: 972-341-3200 or 800-635-7050
Fax: 972-341-3224
The institute conducts research and seeks to provide understanding of the relationship between living habits and health;
offers advice on how to change living habits and develop positive life skills.

Exercise Safety Association
P.O. Box 901
Aurora, OH 44202-0901
Phone: 330-653-5178
Fax: 330-653-5179
Web: www.exercisesafety.com
The ESA is made up of fitness instructors, personal trainers,
health spas, YMCAs, community recreation departments, and
hospital wellness programs; conducts exercise safety and research
programs and maintains a speakers' bureau.

IDEA, the Health and Fitness Source
6150 Cornerstone Ct. E, Suite 204
San Diego, CA 92121
Phone: 619-535-8979 or 800-999-IDEA
Fax: 858-535-8234
Web: www.ideafit.com
IDEA provides continuing education for fitness professionals,
personal trainers, program directors, and club/studio owners;
affiliated with the American Heart Association.

National Athletic Trainers Association
2952 Stemmons Freeway, Suite 200
Dallas, TX 75247-6196
Phone: 214-637-6282 or 800-879-6282

Fax: 214-637-2206
Web: www.nata.org
This 23,500-member organization consists of athletic trainers from universities and colleges, professional sports, military establishments, sports-medicine clinics, and business/industrial health programs. Also compiles statistics and maintains a library of fitness-related materials.

National Collegiate Athletic Association
P.O. Box 6222
700 W. Washington St.
Indianapolis, IN 46206-6222
Phone: 317-917-6222
Fax: 317-917-6888
Web: http://www.ncaa.org
The NCAA consists of university, college, and allied educational athletics associations devoted to the administration of intercollegiate athletics.

National Sports and Fitness Association
1945 Palo Verde Ave, Suite 202
Long Beach, CA 90815
Phone: 562-799-8333
Fax: 562-799-3355
Web: www.nsfa-online.com
This 5,000-member organization is made up of physicians, psychologists, exercise physiologists, nutritionists, and other health and fitness professionals; maintains a speakers' bureau.

National Strength and Conditioning Association
1955 N. Union Blvd.
Colorado Springs, CO 80909-2229
Phone: 719-632-6722 or 800-815-6826
Fax: 719-632-6367
Web: www.nsca-lift.org

This 16,000-member organization is made up of professionals in sports science, athletic, and fitness industries, and promotes conditioning to prevent injury. Also operates a professional certification program.

Profnet
www.profnet.com
Search the on-line database or submit a query to find experts in particular areas; you can also sign up for free e-mail releases about new research and story ideas.

Writers Organizations and Other Resources

Association for Women in Sports Media
P.O. Box #726
Farmington, CT 06034-0726
Phone: 817-390-7409
Fax: 817-390-7210
This 600-member organization is made up of female sports-writers, copy editors, broadcasters, and media relations directors.

Baseball Writers Association of America
78 Olive St.
Lake Grove, NY 11755
Phone: 631-981-7938
Fax: 631-585-4669
Membership in this organization is restricted to sportswriters on direct assignment to major league baseball.

Football Writers Association of America
18652 Vista Del Sol
Dallas, TX 75287
Phone: 972-713-6198
Fax: 972-713-6198
Web: http://www.fwaa.com

This 850-member organization consists of newspaper and magazine writers who cover high school, college, and professional football.

Golf Writers Association of America
10210 Greentree Road
Houston, TX 77042-1232
Phone: 713-782-6664
Fax: 713-781-2575
Web: http://gwaa.com
This 900-member association includes editors and writers who cover golf for newspapers, magazines, and news services.

National Sportscasters and Sportswriters Association
Box 559
Salisbury, NC 28144
Phone: 704-633-4275
Fax: 704-633-4275
This 1,000-member organization consists of sportscasters and sportswriters; operates the National Sportscaster and Sportswriters Hall of Fame.

North American Snow Sports Journalists Association
P.O. Box 74563
2803 West 4th Avenue
Vancouver, British Columbia, Canada V6K4P4
Phone: 604-877-1141
Web: http://www.nasja.org
The association consists of writers of ski-related news, information, and features throughout the United States and Canada.

Professional Hockey Writers Association
1480 Pleasant Valley Way, No. 44
West Orange, CA 07052
Phone: 973-669-8607

Fax: 973-669-8607
The association consists of writers who cover member teams of the National Hockey League.

United States Basketball Writers Association
1000 St. Louis Union Station, Suite 105
St. Louis, MO 63103
Phone: 314-421-0339
Fax: 314-421-3505
This 1,000-member organization includes writers who cover college and professional basketball and players for a variety of media.

Books

Associated Press Sports Writing Handbook
by Steve Wilstein (McGraw Hill, 2002)
Nuts and bolts advice on sportswriting, lots of "war stories," advice from noted sportswriters, and examples of outstanding beat reporting, columns, etc.

The Sports Writing Handbook, Second Edition
by Thomas Fensch (Lawrence Erlbaum Associates, 1995)
Good guide to sportswriting; includes chapters on interviewing, leads, advance articles, sports features, and extensive list of sports teams.

CHAPTER 12

Warm Your Heart

Writing Essays & Personal Pieces

The Basics: What You Need to Know

The overwhelming success of the *Chicken Soup for the Soul* series of books reveals an almost limitless audience for short inspirational and heartwarming pieces. But essays can be humorous, political, or satirical as well. Unlike most other nonfiction fields, essay writers usually forgo the usual query process and submit completed works for consideration. A talented essay writer can command high rates—$2/word and up—from national publications. And because of the nature of the form, essays offer a chance for nonfiction freelancers to write something a little different than usual—and profit from it, too.

Yet essays often appear to be easier to write than they really are. On the following pages, you'll find a wealth of advice from experienced professionals on the keys to writing compelling essays—and getting paid for them as well.

The Nuts and Bolts:
How to Write Essays

Think Beyond Yourself

First and most important, understand that a good essay does more than relate a personal event or share your thoughts, opinions, or feelings with your readers. It can't consist of merely your own experience—it must be broad enough for complete strangers to get something out of it.

"You've got to personalize and at the same time universalize what you're saying, so that other people can relate to what you're saying and agree or disagree with it," says essay writer Susan J. Gordon of White Plains, New York, who has sold essays to publications including *Woman's Day*, *Parents*, *Working Mother*, and *Good Housekeeping*.

"Just telling about an experience in your life, or an insight you had, isn't enough for the majority of editors and readers," agrees Kathryn Lay, a freelancer in Arlington, Texas, who's sold more than 400 essays and personal-experience stories. "You need to find a way others can relate to. Compare your experience to an emotion, a desire, a frustration, a need, or something [else]."

Consider Your Audience

Successful essay writers often think of their audience and consider the message they want to communicate before they begin writing.

"Think about what the market is and who your audience is," says Gordon. "You always have to speak to that particular reader and pay attention to that. What works for me is finding ways to make my personal story meaningful to others. You shouldn't talk about yourself unless you've got a way to let the reader in."

John Lenger of Watertown, Massachusetts, agrees that too

many would-be essayists think only about what *they* want to write, not what people want to read about.

"Each and every one of us is convinced that what we want to say is the most important thing. But that doesn't work when you're talking about a mass audience of thousands or tens of thousands or millions," says Lenger, a freelancer who has sold 100 essays and op-ed (opinion-editorial) pieces during the last 15 years. "Our individual idiosyncrasies are not that fascinating to anyone else."

Instead, think about your audience. "What are our readers thinking? What are our readers feeling? What can our readers identify with? Tell the readers about their problems, not your problems," says Lenger. "If I'm writing a personal essay about one of my experiences, the reason that it's going to be successful is not because it happened to me and I am so important—it's successful because it touches a nerve or a feeling or involves some sort of emotional reaction with the reader."

Sharon Miller Cindrich, a freelancer in Wauwatosa, Wisconsin, always keeps her audience in mind when writing essays. "Your audience has to identify with you and your story—to see themselves or at least part of themselves in the picture," says Cindrich, who writes essays and nonfiction articles.

"Even though the piece may seem to be about me and my experience, my goal is that my audience will immediately see it as a story about themselves. They might see themselves in a new light, with a humorous perspective, or gain a new understanding from it."

Start with a Sideline

While essay writing can be a profitable sideline, few writers can support themselves writing essays alone. As a result, many freelancers write essays for the enjoyment and occasional checks, but rely on nonfiction articles and books to pay the bills. "It's very difficult to make a living just doing essay writing for commercial magazines," says Andrea Cooper, a freelancer in Charlotte, North Carolina. "For one thing, the opportunities at each magazine tend to be much more limited. They'll have the back page essay—and a million articles."

Essays also often take much longer to write than nonfiction articles, and the process may not be as straightforward. "With service pieces [such as how-to articles], you know what they want—10 ways to do this or that. And you do it in a very organized way. You sit down and you get your interviews and put the piece together, and it's done," says Gordon. "Essays take a lot of time, and they can percolate for months. You can't churn them out."

Expand Your Market Awareness

You'll increase your chances of selling and publishing your essays if you look for markets that are a good match for your writing style. While most publications have at least one essay slot, many magazines tend to run the same kinds of pieces over and over. Not surprisingly, a parenting magazine will publish essays on the joys and challenges of raising kids, while a magazine aimed at seniors will run stories that reflect issues its readers face. Consider what the market publishes before you send in your work.

"A fair number of magazines can be pretty conservative in what they take," says Cooper. "One of the lessons I've learned as an essayist is that you really need to look for places that are running pieces that you really admire and that you wish you had written. There are just some places that are going to be a better philosophical match for you.

"Go to the newsstand and see who is publishing what, in terms of the complexity of the subject matter, the tone—and are they essays that require a depth of research or come purely from your own experience? You have to match yourself reasonably well to the publication."

Because the markets for essays may be more limited, it makes sense to look for publications close to home as you begin your essay-writing career. Cindrich first published her essays in the *Chicago Tribune* and a regional publication called *Western Suburban Living*. She now is a regular columnist for *Western Suburban Living* and has branched out to national markets as well.

"Think global, but act local," says Cindrich. "On a national level, you're competing with thousands of writers for a handful of slots. Look into local newspapers, regional mags, newsletters, et cetera, for markets."

Do Your Homework

The great thing about writing essays is that you can simply sit down and write off the top of your head—no research is necessary, right? Wrong. Even for a personal essay, it's often helpful to conduct some research about a topic before you start writing about it. You may use the information you find out as background, or incorporate and weave it into the piece itself. The result can be a more thoughtful and compelling essay.

"I've always found that doing research even for a personal essay is very important," says Cooper. "With a personal essay when you're writing about your own experience, you always run the risk of people looking at this and saying, 'Who cares?' I've found that the research helps me broaden it out somewhat."

Choose Your Material Carefully

If you're writing a nonfiction article, it doesn't really matter how you feel about the subject matter. The fact that ways to cut your household bills or tax-saving tips doesn't excite you is irrelevant. The opposite is true when writing an essay—if you don't have strong feelings about something, your essay will probably be weak. "It's not enough to know about something," says Gordon. "You must also care—and care deeply—about the topic."

Your essay must also offer readers something new. "With

essays, the writing is everything," agrees Cooper. "You have to have original ideas and be able to express them in a way that makes people notice. It's creating an experience for someone who doesn't know you but who will want to be with you because of the experience you're creating together."

Maximize Reprint Sales

While essays do tend to take more time to write than articles, they offer reprint opportunities as well. Pieces that are closely related to recent events may not sell more than once, but essays on evergreen topics can be resold again and again.

For example, Gordon wrote an essay for *McCall's* about her stepfather 15 years ago, and was paid $1,000 for first rights to it. In the years since then, it has been reprinted in the Canadian version of *Readers Digest*, in a textbook, and in *Chicken Soup for the Father's Soul.* All told, she's made more money selling reprints of her essay than she earned in the first place—and she will possibly see it reprinted it again.

Of course, you can only offer reprint rights on essays that you own the rights to, so be sure to read your contracts carefully before signing them. If you sign all-rights contracts or "work-for-hires," you're precluded from reselling your work to other markets such as anthologies.

However, a prestigious clip from a national magazine might be an investment in your portfolio and a chance at exposure, says Cindrich. "So 'selling out' isn't always a bad thing," she adds. "But consider it carefully and weigh the pros and cons before you sell your soul."

Keep an Idea Journal

Sometimes with essays, an idea may spring full-blown, but it's a good idea to keep a running list of potential story ideas. "One thing I encourage is to keep a personal experience journal," says

Negotiate from a Position of Power

If you're known for being able to produce a particular kind of article that a magazine wants, then you can command a higher rate.

For instance, I get $2/word from Marie Claire. And I understand that most writers don't get paid that much.

But I knew they needed these stories, so I said, "This is what other magazines are paying me, so if you want my stories, this is what they cost."

It worked.

—Melba Newsome, Mathews, North Carolina

Lay, who teaches essay writing. "This would include an experience that happens, along with details, senses, and how it affected you, and how it might encourage, challenge, inform, entertain, or surprise readers."

Cindrich often jots notes for essay ideas on her calendar alongside her children's doctor's appointments, after-school activities, and birthday parties. "It doesn't always have to be formal or lengthy," she says. "If I have an idea, I jot down a line or phrase or my thought on my kitchen calendar. I may not come back to it for a while but if I need some ideas, I always know I can browse the notes there."

Another effective way of developing new essay ideas is tying in your subject with a seasonal or regular event. "Be fresh. Take an old idea and turn it around," says Gordon. "Think ahead of upcoming holidays and be seasonal."

Remember that to place essays for holidays like Mother's Day, Easter, Thanksgiving, and Christmas, you'll want to submit your work well in advance. Timing depends on the market, but send event-oriented essays at least six months ahead of time—competition for those slots is high!

Don't Overdo the Details

One of the most difficult parts of writing essays is staying within word count. When you're writing about something that's really important to you, you may not want to leave anything out, but beware: Go overboard with details and you'll lose your readers. Choose wisely and focus on the most important details—the telling details that make the essay. "That's the difference between somebody who is fascinating and someone who is boring," says Lenger. "Practiced storytellers choose just those details that make the story and no more."

It also helps if you know how long the essay will be before you begin writing it. "It helps to structure your story," says Cindrich.

"Research the essay slots or check guidelines if you know you're aiming for a particular publication."

Close the Essay

Make sure that your essay also has a sense of closure. "It's important not to leave your reader hanging. You have to give your reader something to walk away with," says Lenger. "You don't have to come out and say, 'The moral of the story is . . .' That's almost always overdone. But you have to make the connection, complete the thought."

For example, one of Lay's essays was about when she and her daughter rescued a young cardinal and then returned it to the nest so its parents could care for it. "I compared it to the difficulties I had in letting my daughter grow older and fly farther from my own nest," says Lay. "But the only time I mentioned this was in a few brief sentences scattered at the end. Mainly, I relied on the story to draw the reader to the conclusion I had come to during the event."

Tales from the Front: Deborah Shouse

Deborah Shouse, a freelancer from Prairie Village, Kansas, has been writing essays for the past 13 years; they've appeared in markets including *Reader's Digest*, *Woman's Day*, *Family Circle*, *Hemispheres*, and *The Christian Science Monitor*. She offers this advice for essay writers:

- *Write from your heart.* Keep your writing visual—that is, write in scenes, so the reader is anchored and can see and sense what is happening.

- *Keep your essays tightly focused.* The greater the focus, the more chance for emotional impact. Add humor whenever possible. Your goal is to have the reader feel changed by your work.

- *Be persistent.* When you write a piece that you love and feel is good, don't give up. Keep marketing. Shouse has found markets for five-year-old stories after they've been rejected dozens of times. And once they're published, they're often reprinted.

- *Enjoy the process.* "I find this kind of writing wonderful, enriching, and humbling," says Shouse. "Humbling because you have no control over whether magazines want to publish your most wonderful work. Enriching because you have a chance to understand more deeply about yourself and your life. Wonderful because you are doing a kind of writing that when it works can really move and inspire people."

The Markets: Where to Sell Your Work

Essays are unique in that they are not queried; instead, you submit the piece to the editor along with a brief cover letter introducing it.

There are a variety of markets that publish essays and personal pieces, and they vary widely in audience, scope, and focus. Check a publication's back issues to see what types of essays are published, how long they are, and what types of topics are covered, and request a copy of their writers' guidelines before submitting material.

Some of the most popular markets for essays include:

- *Women's magazines.* Women's magazines like *Family Circle*, *Woman's Day*, and *Redbook* have published essays, personal pieces, and humor for years.

- *Men's magazines.* While they don't publish as many essays as the women's publications, men's magazines also publish essays.

- *Parenting publications.* Both national and regional publications run essays, usually having to do with some aspect of parenting or child care, often with a humorous twist.

- *General interest magazines.* Most run essays; a good example is *Newsweek's* long-running "My Turn" column.

- *Regional and local publications.* These smaller markets are often good places for essay writers to gain experience; they offer reprint opportunities as well.

- *Inflight and travel magazines.* Both inflight and travel publications publish essays, ranging in length and scope.

- *Religious publications.* Religious magazines run many essays and personal-experience pieces.

- *Newspapers.* Local, regional, and national newspapers all run op-ed pieces and essays in different sections of the papers.

- *Anthologies.* Books of many short pieces, such as the *Chicken Soup for the Soul* series, purchase rights to essays and publish them in thematic collections.

- *Web sites.* Web sites such as www.salon.com also publish essays and personal pieces.

Other Useful Stuff

Essay writing is a unique skill, but one that can be developed. If you want to write essays, it may be helpful to take a class at your local college or sign up for an on-line course. Joining a writers' group to share and critique your work can help you stay focused and improve your writing skills. There are also a number of books on the craft of essay writing including:

Writing Personal Essays:
How to Shape Your Life Experiences for the Page
by Sheila Bender (Writer's Digest Books, 1995)

Eleven chapters on how to write different types of essays and publish them; includes appendix.

The Essayist at Work:
Profiles of Creative Nonfiction Writers
Edited by Lee Gutkind (Heinemann, 1998)
Nineteen profiles with noted nonfiction and essay writers; gives insight into the craft of essay writing.

Writing Articles from the Heart:
How to Write & Sell Your Life Experiences
by Marjorie Holmes (Writer's Digest Books, 1993)
Eighteen chapters on writing about your personal experiences; includes individual chapters on essays, humor, nostalgia, and memoirs, and information on getting published.

CHAPTER 13

No Place Like It

Writing About Home & Garden

The Basics: What You Need to Know

Do you like to "putter"? Are you known for your homegrown tomatoes? Did you build your backyard deck yourself? If so, as a writer, you're in luck. Entire publications—often called "shelter" magazines—are dedicated to the home and garden niche, and most general interest publications cover these topics as well.

Articles may explain how to landscape your backyard, remodel a bathroom, or maximize your storage space. An interest in these subjects is often a jumping-off point to writing about these specialized areas, and nothing is better than hands-on experience when it comes to pitching story ideas.

Thanks to the practical appeal and increasing interest in home improvement and maintenance, these topics are a lucrative area to specialize in, particularly for writers who have a background in home repair or gardening. Read on to learn how you can turn your do-it-yourself projects into money-making articles as well.

The Nuts and Bolts: Writing About Home and Garden

Use Your Background

As with most specialties, you'll find it easier to break into this area if you already have knowledge or experience with the subject. Take Judy Bistany, for instance, a freelancer from Columbia, South Carolina. She's an interior designer who covers home design as an associate editor for a regional magazine; she is also in a good position to freelance on the side, using her expertise.

Lisa Iannucci, a freelancer in Poughkeepsie, New York, had worked as an editorial assistant at *Home Mechanix*. When she started freelancing, she pitched a story on remodeling and pregnancy, which led to writing a home-decorating column for her local paper. She then used that experience to start writing weekly stories about real estate and home-remodeling subjects for a larger newspaper.

"I basically learned all of it on the job. If I had to do something on mortgages, I learned about it while writing," says Iannucci. "Little by little, I learned more and more. For example, I'm not an interior decorator but I knew where to find the experts." By using her initial knowledge base as a starting point and interviewing experts, Iannucci was soon able to branch into related subjects as well.

Know Your Subject

You needn't be an expert on home repair or on raising prize-winning roses, but you do have to know enough about home and gardening subjects to write about them accurately. "If you're breaking into the interior-design market, you have to understand what design is all about," says Bistany. "You have to understand the depth of it and understand what makes it work."

Arline Zatz, a freelancer in Metuchen, New Jersey, educated herself about garden writing while researching her book *New Jersey's Great Gardens: A Four-Season Guide to 125 Public Gardens, Parks, and Arboretums* (Countryman Press, 1999). Now she's written dozens of gardening-themed articles. "Speaking for myself, I knew very little. I sort of learned on the job," says Zatz. In the course of researching her book, she visited 125 gardens and identified the plants, shrubs, and trees that each site featured. She also researched different types of gardens—herb gardens, English-knot gardens, and All-American Rose Gardens, for example—and included that information in her book.

Keep Up on Trends

Although they may not seem to be, real estate and home design are constantly changing fields. "Homeowners' tastes change often, and what's hot in selling/buying or remodeling now may not be the same six months from now," says Iannucci. "If you are going to write in the real estate or home-decorating field, you need to keep up on the industry trades. You don't need to know exactly what fabric is what, but you should have an idea of what the latest trends are and where to find experts."

Subscribing to trade magazines aimed at real estate agents, builders, interior designers, and residential contractors can help keep you abreast of trends. Also, pay attention to what's happening where you live. Is there an increased interest in water gardens? Are more people adding on to their homes rather than moving? Have upscale condominiums become increasingly popular? Look for evidence of trends on a local level; this can provide you with story ideas as well as possible anecdotes and examples for the articles themselves.

Think Visual

Whether you're writing a piece about interior design or how to prepare your backyard garden for winter, providing photos, illustrations, and other art may be an integral part of the story. "Garden writing is such a visual thing," says Cathy Wilkinson Barash of Des Moines, who's been writing about gardening since 1986. "It's great to have photos that help explain it when you're suggesting a story to somebody, especially as you're starting out. Even if you just take Polaroids of whatever it is, it really helps."

You may use photos to help sell the story idea, and then sell the photos themselves as well. Barash has honed her photography skills over the years and says that it has paid off.

"You get paid more as well; often you get more for the photos than for the story itself," says Barash. Because of this, it's worthwhile to invest in a good camera and take a photography class to learn the basics. And, make sure that if you are selling photos, you retain rights to them so that you can resell them in the future.

Include the Human Element

For a basic how-to piece, your story may be simple in structure. For longer stories or features, you want to focus on specific details or a underlying theme that will bring your story to life. And remember that just because you're writing about interior decorating or gardening doesn't mean that you can't include a human element in your articles.

When Judy Bistany writes about design, she asks the homeowners as many questions about their lives and backgrounds as about their furniture and accessories. "I'll ask questions like, 'Where have you been?' 'Where have you come from?' 'What do you do?'" says Bistany. She also asks who and what sources of inspiration have influenced them throughout their lives, and incorporates that information into the story. "Then I weave the story around their personality and intermix what they've done in their home," she says. "The story is mostly about the person, while the photographic descriptions are mostly about the things."

Write Simply

If you have the ability to break down a task into simple, understandable steps—and describe the steps so that someone else can follow your instructions—consider writing "how-to" articles. These stories don't require a lot of research, but they do require attention to detail. Freelancer Judith Trotksy of Staten Island, New York, has written 40 articles about do-it-yourself projects for magazines including *House Beautiful, Home, Home Mechanics*, and *Home Owner*.

The key is to write clearly, says Trotsky. "Use simple language so that everything you explain is understandable by a 12-year-old," says Trotsky. "This ain't literature. And if there are safety issues involved, be certain to note that and advise appropriate action—like calling a licensed electrician." When pitching ideas, she likes to include photos or mention a specific project as an example of what she'll include in the finished story.

Network with Other Writers

As in other writing fields, there are several organizations aimed at journalists who cover this area. Joining one or more of them will help you get your name out as a specialist in this area and can help you nail new assignments as well. Barash is a member of the Garden Writers Association of America as well as food writing organizations, and has worked as both an editor and a freelancer.

"Many of the jobs I've gotten have been through networking," says Barash. "I moved to Des Moines to be the executive garden book editor for Meredith . . . and then I left that to go

Ditch the Fillers

As soon as you're able, quit writing short pieces.

You'll always make more money per hour on a 1,500-word assignment than on a 300-word assignment.

The short pieces seem to eat a lot more time per word, which translates into lost money.

If you want to break into a magazine, the short pieces are usually the way to do it.

But I try to jump up to the longer pieces as soon as possible, and turn down the shorter assignments.

—Nicole Burnham Onsi, Hopkinton, Massachusetts

back to freelancing. Even the job at Meredith came through a recommendation of a fellow garden writer."

Clearly, it's tremendously important to a freelance career to be networking as much as possible, and specialized writers' organizations provide many excellent opportunities to do that methodically.

Start Small

Writing about home and garden encompasses literally dozens of subjects, including real estate, interior decorating, garden design and maintenance, home improvement and renovations, crafts, and entertaining. If you're new to this area and want to break in, choose a subject that you have personal experience with or knowledge of, and pitch some well-developed ideas to the markets you want to write for.

Many home and garden writers get started writing for local publications to gain experience and build their clips. "For somebody who's just starting out, think local rather than universal. It can easily be worth it," says Barash. "Many regions or towns have a 'penny saver' or a local paper, some of which are syndicated over an area. If they don't have something in gardening, tell them you'd like to write for them. Have experience in gardening, especially on a local level, so you know what you're talking about. And when you don't, know who to go to."

Pitch Seasonal Ideas

If you're writing about gardening, pitch ideas that correspond to the seasons of the year. In the spring, publications run articles about getting your garden started; during the winter, they might focus on indoor gardening topics like forcing bulbs or container gardens, for example. Scout your local community for story ideas, and be on the lookout for possible subjects when you travel. "You could do features on people who are leaders in the community doing things," says Barash. "And if there is a local horticulture society or botanic garden, become a member so you're really up on what is going on."

The same theory applies when you're writing about home-related subjects. Think about topics that tie into seasonal events. You might pitch a story on adding a backyard deck for a spring issue of a homeowners' magazine or a piece on inexpensive holiday decorating ideas for a November or December issue of a women's publication.

Develop a Specialty

Finally, consider crossover topics—stories that touch on more than one subject area—as well. For example, you might write about how to use home-grown herbs in recipes (combining food and gardening) or do a story on ways to get better bargains on antiques while traveling (a mix of interior design, money, and travel).

"Look beyond the obvious topics," says Barash. "Find a niche and go for it, because there are a lot of generalists out there. But if you can become known for a specific area, then people will start coming to you for information."

Barash, the author of nine books, created a unique niche for herself by starting to write about edible flowers years ago, and continues to be recognized as an authority on them. "I've become known as the expert on edible flowers," says Barash. "So, if some magazine is looking for edible-flower information or a recipe or something, I'll give it to them for nothing, making sure that I'm credited, along with my book, *Edible Flowers: From Garden to Palate*." (Fulcrum, 1993)

Tales from the Front: Mary Beth Klatt

Mary Beth Klatt of Chicago has been freelancing since 1995. She's turned a long-term interest in architecture and interior design into a niche, and offers this advice for writers who want to enter this area:

- *Follow your passions.* Klatt has been fascinated with old buildings for years. When she finds one, she'll often do some research to learn about its history and architecture. If the building has an interesting story behind it, she may query it as a possible article to a publication. She's taken a similar approach with interior-design stories, scouting cutting-edge homes, taking photos, and then pitching them as article subjects to her editors.

- *Spot trends.* If you're writing about interior design, you have to keep up on the latest trends, including colors, fabrics, and furniture styles. A lot of it is simply "getting out there" and paying attention to what's happening—fashion trends will often be reflected in interior-design trends a few months later. "When you see the latest handbag on the street, chances are that the color will show up in your living room six months from now," says Klatt.

- *Network.* You have to get out and meet people, says Klatt. As a relatively new design writer, she spent a lot of time at the Merchandise Mart in Chicago, where interior designers display their latest styles. She attended design seminars and introduced herself to interior designers, making valuable contacts.

- *Use photos.* A good camera is one of the best investments you can make. "You definitely want to have scouting shots. A lot of times you can't sell the story without scouting shots, because it's so visual," says Klatt. While they don't have to be expensive photos—they can be Polaroids or digital shots, for example—often the photos will make or break the story.

- *Be accurate.* If you're putting product information or shopping information in a story, it had better be correct. Double-check any information you include.

The Markets:
Where to Sell Home and Garden Writing

More markets cover home and garden topics than you might think. Consider these types of markets when looking for places to sell your work:

- *Shelter and gardening magazines*—so-called shelter magazines focus on home design, décor, interior decorating, home improvement, and other related subjects; gardening magazines cover a range of related topics.

- *General interest magazines*—these magazines often cover aspects of home and gardening; angle and focus depends on the magazine's readership.

- *Women's and men's magazines*—these publications also cover a broad range of home and garden subjects. Women's magazines may focus on interior design and gardening, while men's cover home improvement, remodeling, and repair projects; again, every market is different.

- *Inflight magazines*—while narrower in scope, these publications occasionally include home and garden topics, particularly design, architecture, and noteworthy gardens, buildings, or other locations.

- *Cooking/food magazines*—these publications often cover gardening subjects, as well as a range of home décor, design, and entertaining topics.

- *Travel magazines*—these publications often cover design, architecture, and other home-related subjects; also feature unique buildings and gardens as places to visit.

- *Custom publications*—custom publications often cover home and garden topics because of their wide appeal. Stories range from do-it-yourself projects and simple garden ideas to more complex subjects; check the magazine to determine their slant and coverage.

- *Parenting/child-care magazines*—cover subjects like child-proofing your home, home decorating projects, crafts and activities to do with kids, and the like.

- *Simplicity and nature magazines*—the slant of the publication determines what subjects it covers, but these publications cover home and garden topics as well.

- *National/major newspapers*—cover all aspects of home and garden.

- *Regional/city magazines and newspapers*—like their national counterparts, regional and city publications also cover a broad range of home and garden topics, often with a local angle.

- *Home and garden Web sites*—like their print versions, these markets cover a wide variety of home and garden topics. As with other on-line publications, stories tend to run shorter than in print markets and include quizzes, links to other sites, and other interactive features.

Other Useful Stuff

Looking for sources for home or gardening articles? Consider local ones, especially if they have hands-on experience with the topic you're writing about. Below are some other organizations that may be helpful in researching these types of stories:

U.S. Department of Agriculture Resources

Floral and Nursery Plants Research Unit
3501 New York Ave. NE
Room #217, Administration Building
Washington, D.C. 2002
Phone: 202-245-2726
Fax: 202-245-4575
Conducts research on cultivated woody plants.

Gardens Unit
3501 New York Ave. NE
Room #217, Administration Building
Washington, D.C. 2002
Phone: 202-245-4533
Fax: 202-245-4575
Maintains the arboretum's labeled and documented plant collections, which are the basis for their education and research programs.

U.S. Botanic Garden
245 1st St. SW
Washington, D.C. 20024
Phone: 202-225-8333
Fax: 202-225-1561
Web: www.aoc.gov/pages/usbpage.htm
Collects, cultivates, and grows various plants; identifies botanic specimens and furnishes information on proper growing methods. Also conducts horticultural classes and tours.

U.S. National Arboretum
3501 New York Ave. NE
Washington, D.C. 20002
Phone: 202-245-2726
Fax: 202-245-4574

Performs research on trees, shrubs, and herbaceous plants and educates the public about these plants; library open to the public by appointment.

Associations/Organizations

American Horticultural Society
7831 E. Boulevard Drive
Alexandria, VA 22308-1300
Phone: 703-768-5700 or 800-777-7931
Fax: 703-768-8700
Web: http://www.ahs.org
This organization includes members who are amateur and professional gardeners; affiliated with the American Association of Botanical Gardens and Arboreta. Its mission is to educate and inspire people to become informed and successful gardeners.

American Nursery and Landscape Association
1250 I St. NW, Suite 500
Washington, D.C. 20005-3922
Phone: 202-789-2900
Fax: 202-789-1893
Web: www.anla.org
This 2,300-member organization includes wholesale growers, landscape firms, garden centers, mail-order nurseries, and suppliers; it also maintains a library.

American Society of Interior Designers
608 Massachusetts Ave. NE
Washington, D.C. 20002
Phone: 202-546-3480
Web: http://www.interiors.org
This 30,500 member-organization is made up of practicing professional interior designers and affiliate members in allied design fields.

American Society of Landscape Architects
636 I St. NW
Washington, D.C. 20001-3736
Phone: 202-898-2444 or 888-999-2752
Fax: 202-898-1185
Web: www.asla.org
This organization is a professional society of landscape architects and conducts specialized education and research as well as maintaining a library.

Bio-Dynamic Farming and Gardening Association
P.O. Box 29135
San Francisco, CA 94129-0135
Phone 415-561-7797 or 888-516-7797
Fax: 415-561-7796
Web: http://www.biodynamics.com
Membership consists of farmers, gardeners, consumers, physicians, and scientists interested in organic methods of food production.

Gardeners of America
P.O. Box #241
Johnston, IA 50131-0241
Phone: 515-278-0295
Fax: 515-278-6245
Web: http://dir.gardenweb.com/directory/tgoamgc
Association of home and community gardeners; offers consultation services on horticulture.

Interior Design Society
P.O. Box 2396
High Point, NC 27261
Phone: 800-888-9590
Fax: 336-883-1135
Web: http://www.interiordesignsociety.org

This organization includes 3,000 members and 60 local groups; made up of retail designers, independent designers, and design service firms.

National Gardening Association
1100 Dorset St.
South Burlington, VT 05403-8000
Phone: 802-863-5215 or 800-538-6889
Fax: 802-863-5962
Web: http://www.garden.org
E-mail: dee@garden.org
This organization has 30,500 members and serves as a clearinghouse for home and community gardening information.

Professional Lawn Care Association of America
1000 Johnson Ferry Road, Suite C-135
Marietta, GA 30068
Phone: 770-977-5222
Fax: 770-578-6071
Web: www.plcaa.org
The association includes corporations, firms, and individuals active in the lawn-care business; industry suppliers; and distributors; it conducts research and consumer-education programs and compiles statistics.

Profnet
www.profnet.com
Search the on-line database or submit a query to find experts in particular areas; you can also sign up for free e-mail releases about new research and story ideas.

Writers Associations

Garden Writers Association of America
10210 Leatherleaf Ct.

Manassas, VA 20111
Phone: 703-257-1032
Fax 703-257-0213
Web: http://www.gwaa.org
This organization consists of more than 1,800 professional newspaper and periodical garden writers, photographers, radio and television broadcasters, and book authors in horticultural and allied fields; maintains a talent directory service that refers requests from editors to qualified writers and photographers.

National Association of Home and Workshop Writers
c/o Don Geary
Box 12
Baker, NV 89311
Phone: 702-234-7167
Fax: 702-234-7361
This 90-member organization consists of writers and illustrators of materials on home maintenance and improvement projects, manual skills, woodworking, and do-it-yourself projects and techniques; promotes the sharing of information on publishers and marketing conditions.

CHAPTER 14

Nothing but the Truth

Writing Profiles & True-Life Features

The Basics: What You Need to Know

People want to read about fascinating people. Whether it's the story of a woman who defied all odds and underwent invasive infertility treatments to have children, or a harrowing tale of near-death while on a whitewater rafting trip, the public's appetite for real-life stories is insatiable. Profiles—pieces that introduce readers to notable people—are also popular in both consumer and trade magazines.

Writing profiles and true-life stories that capture readers' attention is an art. The writer must be able to elicit information from his subject(s) and then carefully choose what facts, stories, and insights he'll share, and in what order. Writing these types of stories also gives journalists more latitude with style. True-life dramas in particular are usually told in narrative form, similar to fiction, which offers writers the opportunity for a more creative approach than with a typical nonfiction piece.

If you've always been fascinated by people and what makes them tick, this may be a specialty for you to consider. And if you know someone who has a unique tale to tell, you may already have an "in" when it comes to pitching ideas to markets. Once you know how to locate compelling subjects, draw them out with insightful questions, and make their personalities and experiences come alive on the page, you'll be on your way to developing a lucrative niche in this area.

The Nuts and Bolts:
How to Write Profiles and True-Life Features

Find Your Stories

The first step to writing profiles and true-life stories is finding the people who are the subject of the stories. What makes them worthy of an article? Have they had some extraordinary experience? Did the person face and overcome a common problem? Is she a business leader? Has he changed his community for the better? While everyone's life is interesting on some level, the person featured in a profile or a true-life story must have something unusual or unique that will capture an editor's—and eventually the readers'—attention.

Freelancer Melba Newsome of Matthews, North Carolina, has written dozens of true-life features for a variety of national magazines. She explains that while the stories may differ, they have elements in common.

"Because I write these stories for women's magazines, I know the elements that they are looking for," says Newsome. "Generally, it's triumph over adversity and a story with a good ending—not necessarily a happy ending but some kind of resolution. So I look for women whose stories have those elements."

She adds that her editors also say that they want the subject of the story to be "identifiable," meaning that readers should be able to relate to the person.

Make the Approach

When pitching a profile or true-life feature, you must also consider whether you'll approach your subject before you have the assignment or wait until afterwards. There are several schools of thought on this. Some writers feel that you should always approach your subject before you offer the story to confirm that he or she will participate. Other writers prefer to have the assignment in hand before they contact the person.

"I differ from a lot of people in that I don't contact my subject unless I know that someone wants the story," says Newsome. "Magazines are used to being able to not get a story they want, but the common everyday person isn't used to having a writer call them and say, 'I want to tell your story'—and then having nothing happen."

Because of this, Newsome usually waits to contact a possible story subject until she has a contract for the piece. "I think it carries a lot more weight with them to say, 'I'm a writer and I'm on assignment for *Good Housekeeping*,' rather than saying, 'I'm a writer and I don't know if anything's going to happen, but I would like to try,'" explains Newsome.

Track Them Down

Depending on the story, you may already know the person you're writing about or he or she may be relatively easy to locate. In other cases, you may hear about a person and then have to track him or her down using the Internet and other sources. Newsome reads about possible story subjects in the local paper or sees them on talk television shows, which often mention where they live. She then uses the phone book and the Internet to locate her sources. (There are dozens of search engines and Internet directories for this purpose—see "Other Useful Stuff" at the end of the chapter for more information about them.)

A few quick tips on searching: while search engines vary in terms of how they operate, I've had the most success locating people with sites like www.google.com and www.altavista.com. Try putting in different combinations of the person's name and/or other information you have about them—a city, state, profession, or other criteria.

Internet telephone directories can also be helpful, but the information in them can be out of date. And if you're looking for someone with a fairly common name, you may get too many hits to follow up on. Don't forget to ask your reference librarian if she has any suggestions as well.

Get the Details

When interviewing and researching the story, make sure to nail down details and specific facts. Taping interviews will help protect you if a subject says something and then tries to rescind it later, but ask people for permission to tape before you do so.

During interviews for a true-life feature story, ask plenty of detail-oriented questions so that you'll be able to accurately reprise the story. Ask questions that involve all five senses—sight, sound, touch, taste, and smell. You want to be able to paint a picture with your story, so be prepared to spend lots of time getting background information.

Depending on the story, you may ask things like, "What were you wearing that afternoon?" "What first attracted you to your husband?" "What did your mother say when you told her you had cancer?"

If you're asking about emotionally charged experiences, be prepared to take your time and allow your subject plenty of time to answer and respond.

Streamline the Process

By specializing, I've gotten "as-told-tos" [first-person true-life features] down to an art.

They only require one source, and I can practically write these stories in my sleep—so I get paid a lot of money for relatively little time.

I've also learned what works, what doesn't, and why. So I don't waste a lot of time with proposals that don't go anywhere.

That's a big plus.

—Melba Newsome, Mathews, North Carolina

Do Your Homework

With some types of profiles, your background research may be minimal. But if you're interviewing someone who's well-known in his or her field or is notable in some way, you should prepare in advance.

"Depending on the type of person you're going to interview, you're likely to try to find some old publicity clips that mention this person. If the person has a publicist or is an executive of an organization or company, you'll likely get some handouts about the interviewee's background," says freelancer Sal Caputo of Tempe, Arizona, who writes profiles and covers sports, business, personal finance, and entertainment subjects as well.

"If this profile is an extensive one, then just as you would for any other feature or news story, you're going to want to identify sources you can talk to who can help you understand the subject." While you may only use those interviews as background, you can also use them to verify any information you come across with your subject or through other sources.

"I think it's important to do at least a moderate amount [of preparation], because it really irritates the person you're interviewing if there are key things about them that you don't know," agrees Susanne Alexander, a freelancer from Cleveland, Ohio, who writes profiles as well as business and health pieces. "It can really break down the interview if you come across as being uninformed about them."

Ask the Right Questions—and Establish Rapport

When it comes to the actual interview, your approach may depend on whether the person has been interviewed before. For example, if you're doing a profile, you don't want to cover a lot of the same ground with the person. "Ask yourself why you're doing the profile, and whether other profiles have been done on this person," says Caputo. "This will help you know what's commonly known about the person, so that you can ask questions that probe a little more deeply.

"In the interview, though, always assume that all your research is wrong. As much as you can, quickly verify with the profile subject the truth of the main points you want to make as a result of your research, and get the subject to elaborate on your key points if possible."

When conducting interviews, there is always a give and take involved. For profiles and true-life stories, it's even more important for the interviewee to feel comfortable. One way to do that is to look for ways to connect with the person at the outset of the interview, but you have to be sensitive to the person's response, says Alexander.

"There are times when, in an effort to build relatedness, I might share something personal with myself or an experience that connects in some way with what they're talking about. Then I listen very carefully to how they respond," says Alexander. "If I get very little or no response back, then I won't do that again for the rest of the call."

Get a Sense of the Person

For longer profiles and true-life stories, it's preferable to conduct your interviews in person. "You get a sense from their facial expressions as to what's important to them—and whether they're being straight with you or not," says Alexander. "You can see their mannerisms and expressions, and get a much better feel for what they're enthusiastic about and what they feel strongly about."

Another advantage is that if you meet your subject at home or at work, you're given additional clues to his or her character. "You also definitely get a sense from their environment about what's important to them," says Alexander. "Do they have family pictures up? Do they have fishing trophies?

"If I'm doing the interview by phone, I'll ask them to describe

Reuse Your Research

I revisit my previous stories frequently to see if I can spin them in a different direction.

After all, I already have the sources and I've done the research. So any subsequent assignments should be fairly easy money.

Sometimes, you might find brand-new feature ideas in them. During an interview with a grocery store owner for IGA Grocer-gram [magazine], the man mentioned he was renovating a 100-year-old house into a B&B—with the help of the local high school building trades class.

I remembered that story, and pitched it to This Old House. They bought it.

—cont. on next page

their environment to me. I'll say something like, 'Tell me what's around you, tell me what the setting's like.'" Those details—and the explanations behind them—can help flesh out a story.

Ask questions that go beyond the typical "What has been your greatest business success," or "Would you do anything differently if you had your life to live over?"

"I always try to come up with questions that go to their heart, not necessarily *what* they've done but *why* they've done something," says Alexander. "You want people get a real sense of what's important to them as a person, as opposed as to the surface level of their life."

Listen Up

While it's helpful to have an outline or list of questions you want to ask, it's often beneficial to stray from that list occasionally. "The writer must ask all the pertinent questions and ensure the accuracy of the answers. But a good interviewer is also willing to veer off the subject, if a more engaging one surfaces. And so begins the act of balancing," says freelancer and former magazine editor Kelly Boyer Sagert of Lorain, Ohio.

"My personal solution is this: I research the subject of the interview and jot down thoughts in preparation, but I never create a hard and fast set of questions. I want my interviews to have the flavor of a pleasant yet professional conversation.

"While you're interviewing, the thing I've learned is not to be so set in your ways that you miss an extraordinary story," says Sagert. "Like, if you ask a question and they say, 'Oh by the way, I committed a horrible crime,' and you go on with, 'So, where did you go to high school?'"

Sagert once profiled a retired photographer who donated his time to the local cable television station—a fairly simple piece. At the conclusion of the interview, she asked him about his accent. It turned out that the photographer had been born in Hungary to millionaire parents and had grown up in a mansion with dozens of servants—until the Nazis arrived in Hungary and put his family in a concentration camp. His mother died there, and he and his father came to the United States. When his father broke his back, the teenaged boy was forced to find a job. And photography was all he knew.

"I asked him, 'Can I tell this story?'" says Sagert. "And he said, 'Yeah, if you think anyone cares!'" One offhand question led to a remarkable profile.

Finally, include a general, open-ended question at the conclusion of the interview, says Caputo. "Always ask whether there is something else that you haven't touched upon that they wish to mention," says Caputo.

"Quite often, they have nothing, but every now and again, this question turns up brand-new information that the interview subject, now comfortable with you, would never have mentioned earlier."

Pick a Point of View

When telling a true-life feature, you have to choose whether you'll tell the piece in third person or in first person, also called an "as-told-to." There are advantages and drawbacks with each approach. If you tell the piece in third person, you have more latitude and can share more information. A first-person story may be more gripping, but it will also limit what you can include.

For example, when Newsome wrote a first-person story about a woman who was stranded in the Alaskan wilderness, she could only share the woman's personal experience—she couldn't talk about the rescue parties that were searching for her or share other information, as she could have in a third-person piece.

But for that story, she wanted readers to have a sense of what the woman was going through and her fear that she might not ever be found. Choosing to tell her story in the first person brought those emotions out more convincingly than a third-person piece would have.

Reuse Your Research

—cont. from previous page

Sometimes, you'll rediscover a tiny blurb of info that's worthy of a short.

I wrote a feature for People magazine about a 25-year-old who's cleared 1 million pounds of trash from the Mississippi River. But that story didn't mention his Adopt a Mississippi River Mile program.

So I pitched and wrote a short about that specific program for Field & Stream.

Now, I'm not an outdoors enthusiast. I hadn't been eyeing Field & Stream as a market.

But I thought the idea was a perfect match for the magazine. And the editor agreed.

—Kristin Baird Rattini, Shanghai, China

Pull It Together

Writing the true-life story requires reviewing your interviews and research to determine which moments you want to illuminate in your piece. "The most important thing to remember is when you're interviewing the person, listen for those moments where it tugs at your heart," says Newsome. "When I interview someone, the part that strikes me is the part that strikes the reader. Focus in on those parts that have the drama and be sure to tell that."

Like fiction, true-life stories usually follow a linear form with a beginning, middle, and end. You want to give enough background so that the readers will care about the people involved, tell the story, and finally have a resolution.

When writing profiles, you'll want a mix of running text and quotes from your subject and possibly quotes from others as well. "It's a balancing act between narrative and quotes," says Sagert. "I try to separate what should be quotes and what should be narrative, and pull out the strongest quotes and best words."

With profiles, you want to go beyond simply sharing details about your subject's life—you want conflict and resolution, says Caputo. "If this person has made some dramatic achievement, what obstacles did he or she overcome? If the person was on the fast track all his or her life, it's going to be a pretty dull story, but everybody has setbacks or qualms or phobias," he says.

"These points of weakness or stress—a businessman who decides he wants to be top dog but also wants to give his family plenty of time, and so has to juggle even greater demands than the guy who just puts his family on the back burner—or contradiction and complexity—the producer of a risqué show that's on in prime time, who doesn't let his children watch TV because it's too risqué—these are what you want to illuminate."

Tales from the Front: Kristin Baird Rattini

Freelancer Kristin Baird Rattini who currently lives in Shanghai, China, has written more than 200 profiles as a freelancer for trade and consumer magazines and newspapers. She offers these tips for writers who are new to writing profiles:

- *Don't talk too much.* "There's a fine line. You have to establish a conversation; when it seems more like a conversation instead of an interview, subjects tend to open up more," says Rattini. "But you have to stop yourself from talking too much. This story is about the subject; it's their voice you want to hear, their story you're trying to tell. So zip your lip, and simply listen."

- *Remember the simple courtesies.* Especially, respect your subject's time. Always confirm that this is a convenient time to talk. And always call on time. Rattini was recently thanked profusely by a subject for calling on time. He told her he is interviewed frequently, and how other writers have called as much as a half-hour or hour late with no explanation. He was impressed with her punctuality and professionalism, and gave a much more gregarious interview than she might otherwise have expected.

- *Get under the surface.* "Personal profiles are a format where it's easy to fall into cliché," warns Rattini. "The hero. The martyr. The underdog. While that tagline is often what sells the piece, it will sink the piece if you don't flesh out your subject beyond that label." Dig deep during your interviews so that you can present a well-rounded story rather than just a one-dimensional look at someone.

- *Think outside the box.* If your subject is frequently interviewed, she has developed pat answers that she has at the ready for when those inevitable questions arise. Surprise your subject by asking questions that will jolt her out of her rut.

"When I interviewed Jim Davis [cartoonist who writes the *Garfield* strip] for *Boys' Life*, first I read several previous interviews he'd given," says Rattini. "I saw several answers repeated from one story to another. So I took great care to avoid those ruts. Since I was also interviewing 'Garfield,' I played to Garfield's attitude, knowing he would rise to the occasion. Several times during my interview, after hearing my question, Davis' first response was, 'Great question. I've never thought about that one before.'"

Markets: Where to Sell Profiles and True-Life Features

There's no shortage of markets for profiles and true-life features, ranging from small local publications to national glossies. Nearly every publication features some sort of profiles; keep the market in mind when you pitch a potential story subject, whether it's a simple profile or a dramatic true-life story.

Some of the biggest markets for this kind of writing and related areas of interest include:

- *General interest magazines*—include profiles of business and political leaders, innovators, athletes, other people of note; also publish newsy stories and true-life features

- *Professional and trade journals*—use a lot of profiles of successful people in their respective businesses and industries.

- *Women's and men's magazines*—these magazines profile people who have accomplished something newsworthy, whether they're sports figures, celebrities, or "real people" who have experienced something unusual.

- *Parenting magazines*—include more true-life features, but may include profiles as well, depending on the magazine.

- *Inflight publications*—often include profiles of successful

business executives, analysts and pundits, "movers and shak-
ers," celebrities, and other notables.

- *National/major newspapers*—include a broad range of profiles such as business leaders, sports figures, celebrities, and
the like; also include true-life feature stories.

- *Regional/city magazines and newspapers*—like their national
counterparts, regional and city publications also include a
broad range of profiles of notable local residents, along with
true-life features.

Other Useful Stuff

To write compelling profiles and true-life features, you need excellent interviewing skills and a genuine interest in the people
you're speaking to and writing about. You may also have to use
the Internet and other sources to locate potential story subjects.
Listed below are some Internet resources and books that may be
helpful for freelancers who want to write profiles and true-life
features:

Internet Search Engines

My favorites include:

www.altavista.com
www.google.com
www.infoseek.com

Internet Telephone Directories

While there are dozens to choose from, these are my favorites:

www.anywho.com
www.bigfoot.com

http://people.yahoo.com
www.switchboard.com

Books

Feminine Wiles: Creative Techniques
for Writing Women's Feature Stories That Sell
by Donna Elizabeth Boetig (Quill Driver Books, 1998)
Practical suggestions and examples for selling to the women's
magazine market.

Creative Conversations:
The Writer's Complete Guide to Conducting Interviews
by Michael Schumacher (Writer's Digest Books, 1990)
Good overview of interviewing skills, along with useful tips and
suggestions.

Writing for Story
by Jon Franklin (Penguin Group, 1994)
Practical advice on feature writing, including information-
gathering, structure, and editing.

Creative Interviewing:
The Writer's Guide to Gathering Information by Asking Questions,
3rd Edition
by Ken Metzler (Allyn & Bacon, 1997)
Overview of interviewing techniques, including ways to overcome "interview anxiety," get subjects to open up, and write
profiles.

Broaden Your Horizons

WHILE THIS BOOK FOCUSES ON WRITING and selling nonfiction articles, at some point, you may want to expand your writing career into other areas. Would you like to be a book author? Interested in picking up some corporate work? Or maybe you'd like to reevaluate your career and switch writing fields. As a freelancer, you'll discover there's no specific career track to follow—the path you choose is entirely of your own making.

When you specialize, however, you're more likely to be ready to take advantage of other opportunities. You've already developed an expertise in one or more subjects, which sets you apart from other writers. You can use that knowledge to author books, speak, teach, or write for corporations or businesses.

Sometimes new writing opportunities will fall into your lap; other times, you'll have to seek them out. While there are a variety of lucrative gigs available for talented writers, this chapter includes a brief look at some of the most popular.

Read on for more information about some of the ways you can diversify your writing career—and how to tell if the opportunities are right for you.

Contributing Editorships

You've probably seen names and the phrase "Contributing Editor" (CE) on the mastheads of some of your favorite magazines. Usually the CE is a writer who has an ongoing relationship with the publication. He or she may have been a former full-time staffer or a freelancer; in any case, the writer produces stories for the publication on a regular basis.

Some contributing editors have an agreement to write a certain number of stories for a set amount of money each month; some write as many pieces as the editor needs for that issue; and others receive a retainer regardless of what they produce that month. As a freelancer, it's worthwhile to seek out CE gigs. They offer steady income and the opportunity to develop long-lasting relationships with publications. Having your name on the masthead can lead to other writing assignments as well.

Margaret Littman, a freelancer based in Chicago, has had a number of contributing editor jobs, including at *Crain's Chicago Business*, *Teen*, *Snack Food Magazine*, *Bakery Production*, and *Marketing*, during her freelance career. How did she get them? She simply asked.

"I make sure it is an editor I feel appreciates me—and someone with whom I want to work on a more regular basis," says Littman, who's currently a CE at *Chain Leader*, a trade magazine. "If I get a vibe that they're really appreciative of what I do . . . I've asked to make it more formal."

Littman agrees that there are several advantages to being a CE. Contributing editors often make more money than "standard" freelancers; some magazines have paid her a flat monthly retainer in addition to what she gets for the stories she writes. As a CE, she also knows that she'll be receiving a check at the same time every month, which makes managing her cash flow a little easier.

Another aspect Littman, a former magazine editor, enjoys is the chance to work more closely with the editors on stories. "It's not just querying and then waiting to see if they accept it," she says. "I feel like I have a little more say in shaping the stories, and shaping the section or direction they take. I like that—for me, it's a good compromise. I don't miss editing on a day-to-day basis, but as a freelancer I do sometimes miss the big-picture editing, in terms of thinking and developing a whole package for a story."

If you're going to approach a market about becoming a CE, you should already have a good relationship with the publication. Consider the benefits to the magazine by making you a CE, so that you can make a strong argument in your favor.

"Think about why the editor would want to do this, as opposed to why *you* want it," says Littman. As a contributing editor, you'll always be available for assignments, which will save them time and hassle looking for other writers. If you'll come up with ideas for the editor, show how this will benefit her as well. "If you have an agreement where you're going to come up with the ideas—or maybe 50 percent of the ideas that you're writing—that's another time-saver for them," says Littman. "Point out why it's good for them."

Another plus? While there are no guarantees, contributing editor jobs also tend to be a little more stable than simply freelancing for a magazine.

"You have some job security," says Littman. "If they have to cut back, they'll give something to me before they give something to another freelancer."

The one drawback is that as a CE, the magazine you work for may ask you not to write for any of its competitors. That's one possible trade-off to the relationship, but for most writers, it's worth it.

Love Your Work

Most of all, I think it helps to want to do this so much that you can't imagine doing anything else for a living.

After seven years of full-time freelancing, I'm hooked.

It's hard work, it requires a tough hide, and you can't be shy about promoting yourself and your work.

But it's a great life.

—Kathy Sena, Manhattan Beach, California

Book Authorship

It's not surprising that many nonfiction writers start with magazine articles and continue on to write books. While books take much longer to produce, royalties can provide additional income for years—although sometimes, authors write books for a specific sum in exchange for the copyright rather than for an advance and potential royalties.

Gerry Souter started out as a magazine journalist before moving into video, film, and interactive projects; he then began writing books both on his own and as a coauthor with his wife, Janet. The Arlington Heights, Illinois, native has written books on topics including multimedia services, computers, firehouses, toy trains, and village histories. He says that his varied background has helped him develop expertise in a number of areas.

Rather than developing one niche, Souter has written about many different subjects and says it's important to maintain interest in what you're writing about. "If you're always writing the same subject material all the time, you get dry and flat," says Souter. "With books, you're in the really long format. You can't afford to be flat—you have to be interesting."

"If you start out writing magazine articles, you have to be flexible," says Souter. "Try to write as many different magazine articles as you can, just out of the curiosity of it, because when you get into books, you keep that same philosophy going."

If you're interested in writing books, developing other skills like photography can also help you. You should also start thinking early on how you'll help promote and sell your books.

"One of the key things you can offer publishers is a willingness to promote your book," says Souter. "You will probably be a midlist author—which is the wasteland—and they will not spend a great deal of money promoting your book. But promotion is really important for a book—otherwise it just sits there and does nothing. You have to beat the drum and blow the horn. It's much different than a magazine piece in that respect."

The first step in writing a book is doing background research. You need to make sure you have a good handle on the material and an idea of how long it will take you to write. "With a book, because you're committing to a much bigger project, you have to do a lot of your research before you query," says Souter. "In fact, before you even query a publisher, you'd better make sure you can do the book."

Next, you write a book proposal. A well-researched proposal will help sell your idea, says freelancer Leah Ingram of New Hope, Pennsylvania. Ingram started out writing magazine articles but has written five books as well, including *The Bridal Registry Book* (Contemporary, 1995) and *The Balanced Bride: Preparing Your Mind, Body and Spirit for Your Wedding and Beyond* (Contemporary, 2002).

"The book proposal is always the toughest part," says Ingram. "If you do go from magazine articles to books it can't just be, 'Oh, I wrote about this cool topic and now I want to do a book.' You have to do the legwork to expand it so that it will in fact take up 200 pages. Magazine articles on average run 1,500 words, while every book I've written has been at least 50,000 words. You have to convince the agent or editor that it's more than just a magazine article."

Obviously, the topic that you pitch also affects your chance of getting a book deal. Find a unique niche and show that there's a need for the book, and you're halfway there.

Ingram's first book grew out of an article she wrote for a bridal magazine on offbeat places to register for wedding gifts. "I had more information than I knew what to do with. And while doing the research, I'd found that there were no books on bridal registries, yet every engaged couple registers," says Ingram. In her proposal, she pointed out the lack of books addressing this topic and how her book would be a popular choice for brides and grooms.

Another factor that publishers consider is the author's "platform" and expertise. If you've established yourself in a particular

Forget the Muse

Remember that freelancing is a business. Discipline is more important than inspiration, I think.

I see a lot of beginning writers talking about waiting for "the muse."

I believe that just keeping a regular writing schedule will help you produce far more good writing than you'll ever create by sitting around waiting for a spark of inspiration.

That doesn't sound terribly romantic, but it leads to more published articles—and more checks in the mail.

—Kathy Sena, Manhattan Beach, California

field and have media connections, you're more likely to get a book contract.

"Book editors and book agents all talk in terms of platforms —and we're not talking shoes," says Ingram, who herself has developed a platform as a wedding and gift-giving expert. "They want somebody who has established himself or herself as an expert.

"I'm sure there are plenty of first-time authors who do not have a huge platform, but at least you need to show clips in that area, that you have written about this and that you have contacts in the media who would be interested in the topic, the idea being that you will help market the book," she says

While actually writing a book may seem like a much larger enterprise than writing an article, the process is similar. "It's really not that different from writing a magazine article," says Souter. "You outline what you're going to do, and you gather all your research and your resources together. You've got to make sure that you've got all your resources. It's just like a magazine—except you stretch it out over a few months instead of a few weeks."

To stay on top of your research when writing the book, Souter suggests keeping a separate computer directory and carefully dating, footnoting, and attributing your quotes and other information as you're putting the book together, so you know where they came from.

The bottom line is that writing books takes a much larger time commitment than writing articles, and not every freelancer wants to invest months in a book project. The prospect of advances and possible royalties down the line, however—as well as the desire to create something more permanent—attracts many freelancers to book authorship.

Corporate Writing

One of the most lucrative writing areas for freelancers is writing *for* corporations or businesses—not just *about* them as the subject of articles. The work isn't always glamorous or interesting, but the pay often makes it worthwhile.

When freelancer Polly Campbell of Beaverton, Oregon, started her own PR and freelance business, she did a lot of work for local businesses. "Corporate writing really draws on your writing skills and your ability to connect with people through words," says Campbell.

"It's not about creating something that's a part of you as much as it is creating something that services the client. So you have to always understand the mission at hand and what they're trying to convey, and then figure out a way to diplomatically tell them which style is going to work for them effectively."

If you're interested in writing for corporations, the first step is finding clients. "You have to be in areas where those people are going to go, and you need to dress like them and think like a business person," says Campbell. "When I was focused on corporate writing, I was at the chamber meetings and doing the network lunches. That was the commitment I made, and it paid off. You don't go to those things in jeans and a sweater; you go in a suit. You need to be on the corporate level with them."

While she's phased out most of her corporate work in favor of writing for magazines and newspapers such as *The Oregonian*, she continues to do some business writing because it pays so well. "I will always have one corporate client," she says. "It can give you a stable income, and it helps give me story ideas for freelance things I can do as well. It gets me out in the community and teaches me about things I don't know about, and that fuels my writing."

Of course there can be drawbacks. You may deal with difficult clients, tight deadlines, or unreasonable expectations. One of Campbell's pet peeves is "people who don't know anything about writing, but who will edit your work regardless," she says. "And it's sometimes a challenge to understand what the client needs, because it might not be in alignment with what you think the writing should do."

Lease Out Your Brain

Because freelance writers have to have a sense of marketing if they're going to succeed, I will "rent my brain" for an hourly fee to small business owners who want to brainstorm with someone who is experienced in marketing.

Granted, one reason I can do this is the fact that I ran an advertising/PR firm for a dozen years.

—Barbara Bartocci, Overland Park, Kansas

Teaching

Many writers teach, and vice versa. If you enjoy working with students—whether children, teens, or adults—you may want to explore teaching as a sideline. Sally Stich, a freelancer in Denver, taught high-school and then college students before she began writing 15 years ago. While her freelance income outpaced her salary from teaching long ago, she continues to teach for other reasons as well.

"It's fun to share what you know about writing with your writing students. And I think it keeps me interested in what I'm doing," says Stich. "And you never know who you're going to meet who has a good story—or who knows someone who would end up to be an anecdote or a story . . . the more people you talk to, the more contacts you have and the more you can find something you never expected."

The biggest drawback of teaching? "Grading papers is a drag," says Stich. "On the plus side, it gives you great sympathy for editors!"

You don't have to have teaching experience to become an instructor, though. If you're interested, start out small. Talk to your local continuing-education district office, community college, or other adult-program provider about offering a course for writers—or on another specialized subject you feel qualified to write about.

"Be really well-prepared, "says Stich. "Start at a level where you're comfortable. It might be teaching at the local community college, but cut your teeth with material and a venue that makes you feel totally comfortable."

Those types of teaching jobs won't pay much, but they'll allow you to develop your skills and hone your materials. As you go on, you can move on to higher-paying institutions.

Most writers who teach as well, however, aren't in it for the money. They do it because they love it. "There is nothing in the world that feels better than being in front of a group of people who want to do what you do, and talking about something you love," says Stich. "It feels really good."

Speaking

Not every writer enjoys the thought of standing at a podium before an audience. For those who do—and have a platform as well as natural speaking skills—speaking can be a lucrative sideline.

Ed Gordon, an author, freelance writer, and speaker from Chicago, has turned his business and educational expertise into a successful speaking career. "A lot of writers are shy and don't have the skill set [to be a successful speaker]," says Gordon. "But a lot of speakers don't have any content, so I fill a very useful niche."

Gordon developed his speaking talent over many years, and suggests that writers who are interested in this field hone their presentation skills. "You have to learn how to become a professional speaker," says Gordon. "If you don't have opportunities to give public presentations now, you have to get them and you have to develop those skills.

"Join Toastmasters, join volunteer organizations, and volunteer to give presentations. You can also join a group like National Speakers Association." While content is important, you also need to discover ways to improve your voice tone, your ability to project your voice, and master other mechanics of speaking.

Consider what your "platform," or specialty, will be and how you'll use this to market yourself. "That's where journalists have a tremendous advantage," says Gordon. "They have content, and they've done a lot of research already. If you want to be a professional speaker, you have to be an expert in something. The value of journalists doing this is that many are experts in a particular area. And they've published. Even if they only have articles written, they're good handouts for a program."

Project an Image of Success

I have always expected to make a fine living by writing.

I've always bristled at the starving writer mentality, and it has paid off—literally and figuratively.

I just love to tell people that I couldn't take a job in the corporate world because I'd have to take a 50 to 70 percent pay cut.

Usually, they're shocked. "Wow, I didn't know writers made that kind of money."

My response: "I do."

—cont. on next page

While you may be good at it, speaking is an extremely competitive field, notes Barbara Bartocci, a freelancer and professional speaker based in Overland Park, Kansas.

"Just as there is giant leap between people who want to be writers—and are trying to be writers—and actually writing for major magazines, there is a giant leap between speaking to your local Rotary groups and actually getting paid for speaking," says Bartocci. "Probably the only field I know that is as competitive as writing is speaking."

Bartocci gives a variety of types of speeches and has also worked for seminar companies in the past. Companies like the American Management Association, Padgett-Thompson, Skillpath, and Fred Pryor use speakers to present seminars on business-related topics throughout the country; working for one of these companies is an excellent way to gather a lot of experience.

"The seminar companies will send you out to do public seminars, and you travel four to five days a week. You're in five cities in five days," says Bartocci. "It's pretty much a killer schedule, but a lot of people want to do it.

"To be considered for one of these seminar companies, you want to contact the person that handles contract speakers at the company. Very often they require a videotape of you doing a presentation, and you have to be able to do the kinds of topics that are hot for the seminar company."

But there is a huge advantage to working for seminar companies, says Bartocci. "There is no better way to get experience," she says. "You learn things when you are on the road that there is no way you could learn sitting in your office and speaking to the Rotary club."

Consulting

As a writer, you've developed a body of knowledge about a variety of subjects. Why not get paid for all that information and expertise you've accumulated?

Tom Brosnahan, a full-time travel freelancer based in Concord, Massachusetts, recently added consulting services to his résumé. He performs itinerary planning, on-the-ground guidance (like leading a Discovery Channel scouting team around Turkey looking for filming locations), guidebook author recruitment, and other services for clients.

"Anyone with expertise can act as a consultant; anyone who has written a book or lots of articles on the same topic is an expert (to most of the world)," says Brosnahan. "Your expertise is the important thing, but the way you sell yourself is what actually gets you an income from your expertise."

To be a successful consultant, you can't be bashful. "If you know your stuff, act that way and potential clients will take you at your word and pay accordingly," says Brosnahan. He suggests consultants do the following:

- Set up a different persona for yourself as "expert consultant" as opposed to your identity as a writer.

- Describe your expertise and its usefulness accurately and in detail.

- Create professional business cards and letterhead (in addition to the ones you already use for your writing business).

- Market your services whenever you have the opportunity.

- Put up a simple Web page as an Internet calling card.

- Work out a rate schedule so you know what to charge when someone asks.

Also, be sure to set your prices high enough. "If someone really needs the expertise you have, it means you can solve a problem for them. They are willing to pay good money for this," says Brosnahan. "A decent starting rate is $100 per hour, plus

Project an Image . . .

—cont. from previous page

Interestingly, the image of success breeds success.

Any psychologist will tell you that people naturally gravitate toward other people who are successful.

I always try to present the image that I am very successful (and I think that I am by almost any measure) and that I am busy. I value my time, so editors and corporate types must value my time, and they must pay for the professionalism and my level of expertise.

I'm not supplying words, I'm supplying knowledge. Particularly in the corporate world, I'm not only a writer, I'm a communications consultant.

Believe me, this thinking rubs off.

—Sam Greengard, Burbank, California

expenses. And professional consultants with first-rate business credentials earn $1,500 to $2,000 per day and up!"

Decide in advance whether you will bill by the hour, half-hour, quarter-hour, or minute; whether you will require a time minimum (like two hours or a half-day, for example), and whether you will charge for time spent traveling. And be ready to write a detailed proposal with an estimated total fee for larger projects or to answer questions from potential clients.

"In short, when dealing with businesses, be businesslike and confident in your skills and expertise, and your clients will too," he adds.

So Many Choices, Too Little Time?

Finally, remember that as a freelancer you can create your own career. There's nothing wrong with dabbling in different areas to help you stay marketable and ensure a steadier flow of income—and the type of work you do may change as well.

My first two years as a freelancer, I did a lot of work for small businesses, in part because I needed the money to help pay my bills. The last couple of years, I've focused primarily on magazine work, but I've continued to do some occasional copywriting and other writing projects for local graphic designers. (They do the layout and design; I write the copy.) It's a nice change of pace from writing articles in my usual niche about nutritional pitfalls and vaginal health, and checks usually come much more quickly than with magazines.

Each freelancer's career goals will be different, and the beauty of freelancing is that you can adapt your career to meet those goals. When I started freelancing, my overriding goal was to not have to return to the law—and I wanted to make a living as a writer as well. For me, that meant focusing on several lucrative writing specialties.

Then I decided I wanted to make a good living at it. Then I realized I wanted to spend more time teaching and speaking because I enjoy both.

Then I decided I wanted to start writing books in addition to articles.

Then I decided I wanted to start writing fiction again.

Because I freelance, I can let my current priorities dictate the way I spend my time. No, I can't quit writing for magazines and just write the great American novel full-time (not if I want to continue to make a living, that is.) But I can set aside some time every week to work on projects that are creatively fulfilling to me even though they don't bring in any money (yet). That freedom is one of my favorite things about this business.

If you're going to freelance and support yourself, you're probably going to have to take on work that doesn't particularly interest you at one time or another. When you have bills to pay, that's the reality.

But take advantage of the fact that you can pick and choose the assignments you take and the way you spend your time. By spending as much time as you can on the work you enjoy, you'll enhance your overall satisfaction with your freelance career and your life as a whole.

More Resources for Writers

I've included some books, associations, and market guides that freelancers should find useful. This isn't intended to be an all-encompassing list, but it does offer some helpful resources to help you develop your career.

Books: Writing for the Internet

Online Markets for Writers:
How to Make Money by Selling Your Writing on the Internet
by Anthony Tedesco and Paul Tedesco (Henry Holt, 2000)
Covers 200 on-line markets and advice on how to write for Web sites, procedures, etc.

Writing.com:
Creative Internet Strategies to Advance Your Writing Career
by Moira Allen (Allworth Press, 1999)
Excellent resource that explains how to use the Internet to

research, find markets, sell your work, and promote yourself on line; includes extensive list of on-line resources.

Books: Writing for Magazines

Magazine Writing That Sells
by Don McKinney (Writer's Digest Books, 1994)
Good overview of queries, interviewing, writing techniques, etc.

How to Be Successfully Published in Magazines
by Linda Konner (St. Martin's, 1990)
Some tips and interviews with editors and successful freelancers.

Handbook of Magazine Article Writing
Edited by Jean Fredette (Writer's Digest Books, 1988)
Somewhat dated, but lots of information about all aspects of magazine writing.

How to Write Irresistible Query Letters
by Lisa Collier Cool (Writer's Digest Books, 1990)
Nuts and bolts on those all-important queries.

Query Letters/Cover Letters: How They Sell Your Writing
by Gordon Burgett (Communication Unlimited, 1985)
More guidance on query letters.

You Can Write for Magazines
by Greg Daugherty (Writer's Digest Books, 1999)
Pretty good guide for beginners, with practical tips and suggestions.

Sell and Resell Your Magazine Articles
by Gordon Burgett (Writer's Digest Books, 1997)
Fourteen chapters on the basics of writing queries, researching stories, and reselling your work.

Writing Articles About the World Around You
by Marcia Yudkin (Writer's Digest Books, 1998)
The 12 chapters in this book cover writing about what you know, along with advice on querying, research and interviewing, and building your freelance career; includes resource section and glossary.

Books: Business and Corporate Writing

The Copywriter's Handbook
by Robert Bly (Henry Holt, 1985)
A little dated, but still an excellent source for writing print ads, brochures, and other sales-oriented writing.

Secrets of a Freelance Writer: How to Make $85,000 a Year
by Robert Bly (Henry Holt, 1988)
Good advice on getting started, marketing your services, and running your freelance business.

Words at Work
by Susan Benjamin (Addison-Wesley, 1997)
Excellent advice on business writing; includes pointers on grammar, proofreading, and editing.

The Well-Fed Writer:
Financial Self-Sufficiency as a Freelance Writer
in Six Months or Less
by Peter Bowerman (Fanove Publishing, 2000)
Good overview of writing for corporations and business; lots of practical suggestions and samples; includes how to freelance full-time, find clients, sell yourself, and the like.

Books: General

Writer's Digest's Handbook of Making Money Freelance Writing
by Amanda Boyd (Writer's Digest Book, 1997)
Excellent; covers nearly all types of writing opportunities and
provides advice on setting up your office, staying motivated, etc.

Write More, Sell More
by Robert Bly (Writer's Digest Books, 1998)
Excellent resource; lots of tips on increasing productivity and
making more money.

How to Open and Operate a Home-Based Writing Business
by Lucy Parker (Globe Pequot Press, 1994)
Excellent resource; covers most nuts and bolts of starting a freelance business.

Grammatically Correct
by Anne Stilman (Writer's Digest Books, 1997)
Good guide to punctuation, spelling, style, usage, and grammar.

Find It Fast
by Robert I. Berman (Harper Collins, 1997)
Good guide to basic research skills; covers on-line sites as well.

*J.K. Lasser's Taxes Made Easy for Your Home-based Business
(Fourth Edition)*
by Gary W. Carter (John Wiley & Sons, 2001)
Excellent plain-English guide to what you need to know about
taxes, deductions, and the like.

National Writers Union Freelance Writers' Guide
Edited by by James Waller (National Writers Union, 2000)
Good resource that provides information about different mar-

kets and rates; includes first-person accounts of successful free-lancers.

Too Lazy to Work, Too Nervous to Steal:
How to Have a Great Life as a Freelancer
by John Clausen (Writer's Digest Books, 2001)
Interesting read on the freelance life; includes anecdotes from other freelancers and general advice on the pros and cons of free-lancing.

The Writer's Essential Desk Reference
Edited by Gloria Tennant Neff (Writer's Digest Books, 1991)
Comprehensive guide to writing, researching, business and copyright issues; includes resource information.

Writer's Associations

Associations devoted to particular niches are included in individual chapters. Some of the major associations for professional freelance writers as a whole include:

ASJA
1501 Broadway, Suite 302
New York, NY 10036
Phone: 212-997-0947
Fax: 212-778-7414
Web: www.asja.org
This 1,100-member organization includes freelance writers of magazines and books. (Shameless plug: I'm a member of ASJA, and it's been an invaluable resource for my career.)

Authors Guild
31 E. 28th St.
New York, NY 10016

Phone: 212-563-5904
Fax: 212-564-5363
Web: www.authorsguild.org
This 8,100-member organization consists of professional book and magazine writers.

National Writers Union
113 University Place, 6th Floor
New York, NY 10003-4527
Phone: 212-254-0279
Fax: 212-254-0673
Web: www.nwu.org
The NWU consists of freelance writers, journalists, authors, and other writers.

Market Sources

While *The Writer's Handbook* and *Writer's Market* have long been considered the premier market guides for freelancers, they omit thousands of magazines and newspapers that purchase freelance material. Check out these sources for possible markets; they should be on reserve at your local library:

Bacon's Magazine Directory and *Bacon's Newspaper Directory*
(Primedia Information Inc., annual)
Bacon's includes 70,000 magazines and newspapers, divided under subject headings. (Bacon's also publishes a *TV/Cable Directory* and a *Radio Directory*.)

Gale Directory of Publications and Broadcast Media
(Gale Group, annual)
This multi-volume series is updated annually and includes over 54,500 newspapers, magazines, journals, and other periodicals, subdivided by city and state.

The Standard Periodical Directory
(Oxbridge Communications, annual)
The SPD lists more than 75,000 U.S. and Canadian publications by subject.

Standard Rates and Data Service
Consumer Magazine Advertising Source
(Standard Rate and Data Service, February 2002)
SRDS publishes different volumes for businesses to use when purchasing advertising, including ones devoted to newspapers, radio stations, TV/cable, and direct marketing. The consumer volume is published monthly.

Writer's Market: 8,000+ Editors Who Buy What You Write
Edited by Katie Struckel-Brogan (Writer's Digest Books, annual)
Includes book and magazine markets and information about freelancing.

The Writer's Handbook
Edited by Elfrieda Abbe (The Writer Books, annual)
Includes 3,300 markets and 50 articles about the how-tos of writing and freelancing.

The Writer

The Writer was founded in 1887 by two reporters from the *Boston Globe.* Their mission was to publish a magazine that would be "helpful, interesting, and instructive to all literary workers." The magazine soon became an essential resource for writers, publishing articles in the first half of the 20th century by literary luminaries such as William Carlos Williams, Wallace Stegner, Sinclair Lewis, William Saroyan, Daphne du Maurier, and many others.

After a long editorial tenure into the latter half of the 20th century by A. S. Burack and then Sylvia K. Burack, Kalmbach Publishing Co. purchased the magazine in the year 2000, along with its affiliated line of books on writing fiction and nonfiction, and moved the editorial operations from Boston to Waukesha, Wisconsin, a suburb of Milwaukee.

Continuing its long heritage of more than 110 years of service now into the 21st century, *The Writer* magazine continues to be an essential resource for writers, providing advice from our most prominent writers, featuring informative articles about the art and the business of writing.

It is dedicated to helping and inspiring writers to succeed in their endeavors and to fostering a sense of community among writers everywhere.

More information on *The Writer,* with current articles and other resources, can be found online at the Web site http://www.writermag.com.

—Elfrieda Abbe, Editor
The Writer